OXFORD
MYTHS AND LEGENDS

∾

English Fables and Fairy Stories
Irish Sagas and Folk-tales
Scottish Folk-tales and Legends
Welsh Myths and Legends

SCOTTISH
FOLK-TALES AND
LEGENDS

SCOTTISH
FOLK-TALES AND
LEGENDS

Retold by
BARBARA
KER WILSON

Illustrated by
*JOAN
KIDDELL-MONROE*

Geoffrey Cumberlege
OXFORD UNIVERSITY PRESS
1954

Oxford University Press, Amen House, London E.C.4

GLASGOW NEW YORK TORONTO MELBOURNE WELLINGTON
BOMBAY CALCUTTA MADRAS KARACHI CAPE TOWN IBADAN

Geoffrey Cumberlege, Publisher to the University

First published
1954

*Printed in Great Britain by Richard Clay and Company, Ltd.,
Bungay, Suffolk*

'Storys to rede ar delitabill'
John Barbour, 'The Brus', Book I

ACKNOWLEDGEMENT

The author wishes to acknowledge as her
chief source of material Campbell's collec-
tion of Gaelic folk-lore, 'Waifs and Strays
of Celtic Tradition'.

CONTENTS

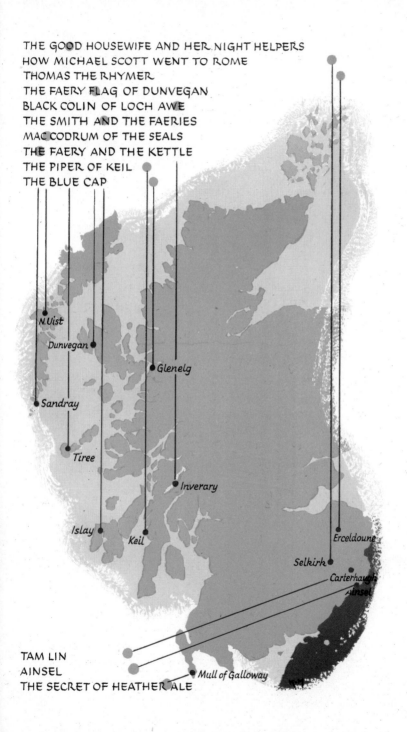

N.Uist

Dunvegan

Glenelg

Sandray

Tiree

Inverary

Islay

Keil

Erceldoune

Selkirk

Carterhaugh

Ainsel

Mull of Galloway

MacCodrum of the Seals

BEFORE the first sailors turned the prows of their
ships seawards to discover what lay beyond their
own homelands, the King and Queen of the sea
dwelt below the waves in peace and happiness. They
had many lovely sea-children, brown-eyed and straight
of limb, who spent the livelong day playing with the
wild sea-horses and swimming through the groves of
purple sea-anemones that grow on the ocean bed. They
loved to make music, these fabulous people who lived in
the sea, and wherever they went there was a sound of
singing like the laughing of the waves.

But one day a great sadness came to the King of the sea
and his carefree children, for the Queen their mother
fell ill and died, and was buried with much sorrowing
among the coral caves of their kingdom. And when she
had gone, there was no one to look after the sea-children,
to comb their beautiful hair and lull them to sleep with
soft sea-music. The King saw their uncombed hair that
hung like the matted seaweed, and he heard them tossing
restlessly at night when they could not get to sleep; and

he thought to himself that he should find a new wife to take care of his children.

Now in the dark sea-forest there lived a strange sea-witch, and it was she whom the King asked to be his new wife, although he felt no love for her, for his heart was buried in the coral caves where his dead Queen lay. The sea-witch thought that it would be a fine thing to be Queen of the sea and rule over such a vast kingdom; and so she consented to marry the King, and became the stepmother of the sea-children. But she was a bad stepmother, for when she saw the brown eyes and straight limbs of the sea-children, she was jealous of their beauty, and resentful that anyone more lovely to look upon than herself should dwell in the sea.

One day she went back to her dark sea-forest and picked the evil yellow berries of the sea-grape that grew there. From these she distilled a magic potion, and wished a cruel enchantment upon the sea-children. She wished that they should lose their straight-limbed bodies and be changed into seals. As seals she wished that they should swim through the sea for ever, except for one day each year, when they could regain their own shapes from sundown to sundown.

This magic came upon the sea-children as they played with the wild sea-horses and wandered among the groves of purple sea-anemones that grow on the ocean bed. Their bodies thickened and lost their shape; their lovely arms were turned into clumsy flippers; and their fair skins were overcast with silken coats of grey and black and golden brown. But they still kept their soft brown eyes, and still they were able to make the music that they loved.

When their father discovered what had happened, his anger against the wicked sea-witch was very great, and he banished her to live in her dark sea-forest for ever.

But he could not undo the magic she had wrought. Then the seals who had once been sea-children sang their lament that they could no longer stay with their father in the place where they had once been happy, but could now be happy no longer. And sorrowfully the old King watched them swim away.

For a long, long time the seals travelled far over the seas. Once a year, from sundown to sundown, they would find a strip of shore concealed from human eyes, and here discard their silken skins of grey and black and golden brown, and step forth in their old, lovely shape. But their sport and playing on the shore never lasted long, and at the second sundown they would put on their skins again and slip back into the sea.

Men say that the seals first came to the Western Isles as secret emissaries from the courts of the Norse kings of Lochlan. Whatever the truth of this may be, it is certain they grew to love this misty western coast, for to this day you may see them as they linger round the Isle of Lewis; or at Rona, which is the Isle of the Seal; or in the Sound of Harris. The people of the Hebrides learnt the legend of the sea-children, and it was known that for one day of the year a man might come across them as they made sport on a strip of shore from sundown to sundown.

It happened that there was once a fisherman called Roderic MacCodrum, of the Clan Donald, who lived by himself on the Isle of Bernerary, in the Outer Hebrides. One day he was walking along the shore where his fishing-boat lay when he heard a sound of singing coming from a group of rocks near by. Cautiously he approached the rocks and peered over the top of them. There before his eyes was a group of sea-children taking their pleasure until the sun went down for the second time. Their long hair streamed behind them as they played, and their eyes were alight with joy. He did not look long, for he knew that the seals were shy of mortal men. But as he turned to go back, he caught sight of a heap of silken skins—grey and black and golden brown—lying on a rock by his side, where the sea-children had discarded them. He picked up one of golden brown that shone with the brightest sheen of all, and he thought to himself that it would be a fine trophy to take back to his shore-side cottage. So he took it with him when he went, and hid it for safe keeping above the lintel of his cottage door.

Now shortly after sundown that evening, as Roderic was mending his fishing-net before his hearth-side, he heard a strange sad noise outside the cottage door. When he looked out, there stood the fairest woman he had ever seen. She was straight of limb, and her eyes were brown and soft. She wore no garment on her white-skinned body, but her gold-brown hair fell thickly down and hid her comeliness.

'Oh, help me, help me, mortal man,' she pleaded. 'For I am a hapless daughter of the sea. I have lost my silken seal skin, and may never return to my brothers and sisters until I find it again.'

Even as he invited her over the threshold of his cottage and gave her his plaid for a covering, Roderic knew full well that this lovely child of the sea was none other than the owner of the skin of golden brown that he had stolen away from the shore that morning. He had only to reach up to the lintel, take down the hidden seal skin, and she would be free to swim away and rejoin her brothers and sisters of the sea. But Roderic looked at her as she sat by his hearth-side; and he thought how pleasant his life would be if he could keep this fair seal woman as his wife, to cheer his loneliness and bring joy to his heart. So he said:

' I cannot help you to find your silken seal skin. I doubt some man came by and stole it as it lay upon the shore—and by now he will be far away. But if you will stay here and consent to be my wife, I will honour you in my home and love you all my life.'

The Sea King's daughter lifted her brown eyes full of sorrow to the fisherman's gaze.

' If indeed my silken skin has been stolen and there is no hope that I may ever recover it, then I have no choice but to remain with you and become your wife,' she said. ' For I could hope for no greater kindness than that you have shown to me, and I should be afraid to venture into the mortal world alone.'

Then she sighed for the life of the sea that she thought she would never know again.

' But I would fain be with my brothers and sisters of the sea, who will wait for me and call my name in vain.'

The fisherman's heart smote him at her distress, but he was so enchanted by her beauty and her gentleness that he knew he could never let her go.

For many years Roderic MacCodrum and his fair seal wife lived in the cottage by the shore, and many children were born to them: children with gold-brown hair and soft voices for singing. And the people who lived about that lonely isle called Roderic ' MacCodrum of the Seals ', because he had taken a seal woman to be his wife; and his children they called ' the Children of MacCodrum of the Seals '. Throughout this time the Sea King's daughter remembered always her great sorrow. She would walk alone by the shore, listening to the *ceol-mara* that is the music of the sea and the *gait na mara* that is the laughter of the waves. And sometimes she would glimpse her brothers and sisters as they swam by the shore, and sometimes she would hear them calling, calling the name of their long-lost sister. And

B

she wished she might join them again with all the longing in her heart.

There came a day when Roderic set out as usual for his fishing, taking fond leave of his wife and children. But on the way to his boat a hare crossed his path, which is a sure sign of ill-luck. Roderic was in two minds whether to turn back or not after this unlucky portent; but he glanced at the sky and said to himself:

'It is only a bit of windy weather that will be my ill-luck today; I have known plenty of storms blow up over the sea before now,' and he went on his way.

He had not been gone long when the wind did blow up. It whistled over the sea, and it whistled round the cottage on the shore where his wife and children were left behind. The youngest child was out on the shore, putting shells to his ear to listen to the sea-music that he loved, and his mother called to him to come inside. Just as he stepped across the threshold the wind blew an even fiercer blast, and the cottage door banged shut with a clash that set the turf thatch a-shuddering. And dislodged at last from the lintel where it had lain hidden ever since Roderic first placed it there for safe keeping, down fell the silken seal skin that belonged to his fair seal wife.

Never a word she spoke aloud against the man who had kept her there against her will for all the long, long years that had passed. But she put off her mortal's clothes, and she clasped the seal skin to her. Then she took one farewell of her children and went down to the sea. And there, while the wild sea-horses frolicked off-shore, she clad herself in her skin of golden brown and swam out across the water. Soon she turned to gaze her last upon the little cottage where she had perhaps known a little happiness in spite of her unwillingness to dwell there. And along the frothing line of surf that rolled in from the great Atlantic she saw her children standing forlorn upon the shore. But the call of the sea was stronger for her than the cry of her earth-born children; and far, far away she swam, singing for joy and happiness as she went.

When Roderic MacCodrum came back from his day's fishing, he found an open door upon a cottage deserted for ever of a woman's care, with no sign of a peat-fire flame in the hearth to welcome his return. Fear filled his heart, and he reached up to the lintel of the door. And when he discovered that the seal skin had gone, then he knew that his lovely wife had returned to the sea. Great was his grief as his weeping children told him how their mother had taken but one farewell and left them alone upon the shore.

'Black was the day that a hare crossed my path as I went to my boat,' sorrowed Roderic. 'For the wind blew strong, and I had but an ill day's fishing; and now this great calamity is fallen upon me.'

He never forgot his fair seal wife, but grieved for her all the days of his life. And remembering that their mother had been a seal woman, for ever after that time the sons of Roderic MacCodrum, and their sons after them, were careful never to disturb or harm any seal that they might see. And they were called the Clan Mac-Codrum of the Seals, which became known throughout North Uist and the Outer Hebrides as a sept of the Clan Donald.

Thomas the Rhymer

ERCILDOURNE is a hamlet that lies in the shadow
of the Eildon Hills. Here in the old days there
lived a man called Thomas Learmont, who was no
different from his neighbours except for the fact that he
loved to play upon a lute, as the wandering minstrels
used to do.

One summer's day Thomas shut his cottage door
behind him and set out with his lute under his arm to
visit a crofter who dwelt on the hill-side, thinking that
the journey would not take him long if he stepped out
with a good pace over the heather. But a brilliant sky
shone overhead, and by the time he reached Huntlie
Bank, at the foot of the Eildon Hills, he felt sufficiently
sun-wearied to rest himself in the leafy shade of a great
tree. Before him lay a small wood, full of green-
cloistered pathways; and as he gazed into its cool depths
and plucked idly at his lute strings, he heard above his
own music a distant sound like the trickle of a hill-side
stream. Then he started to his feet in amazement; for
down one of those green pathways rode the fairest lady
in the world.

She wore a robe of grass-green silk and a mantle of grass-green velvet, and her bright hair hung loosely down upon her shoulders. Her milk-white horse moved gracefully through the trees, and Thomas saw that on each tuft of its mane hung a tiny silver bell, whose tinkling he had mistaken for the trickle of a hill-side stream.

He pulled off his cap and fell down on one knee before the lovely rider, who reined in her milk-white horse and bade him rise.

' I am the Queen of Elfland, come forth to visit thee, Thomas of Ercildourne,' she said.

Then she smiled and held out a slim hand for him to help her dismount. He flung the horse's bridle over a thorn bush and led her to the shade of the great tree, caught fast in the spell of her pale, unearthly beauty.

' Play your lute to me, Thomas,' she said; ' fair music and green shade go well together.'

So Thomas took up his instrument again, and it seemed as though he had never before been able to play such lilting tunes. When he had finished, the Elf Queen showed her pleasure.

' Let me reward you, Thomas,' she urged him. ' Ask me some favour that I may grant you.'

Then Thomas, greatly daring, seized both her white hands in his.

' Let me kiss your lips, fair Queen,' he implored her.

The Queen did not draw away her hands, but smiled and said: ' If you kiss my lips, Thomas, then you must surely fall into my power. You will be bound to serve me for seven long years, through weal or woe as it may chance.'

' What are seven years to me ? ' replied Thomas. ' It is a penalty I would gladly pay.' And he pressed his mouth to the Elf Queen's lips.

Then the Queen sprang up, and Thomas knew that he was bound to follow her wherever she might lead him. Yet still the love enchantment was strong upon him, and he did not regret his bold request, although it was to cost him seven years of his mortal life. She mounted her milk-white steed and bade Thomas vault up behind her; and then, while the silver bridle bells rang sweetly, they sped on through green glades and over heathery slopes, travelling swifter than the four winds of heaven, until they reached a strange countryside, where the Queen alighted and told Thomas they would rest for a little while.

Thomas looked about him curiously, knowing it was no mortal ground on which they stood. A wilderness of curling bracken was behind them, trackless as the sea; but ahead, three roads branched off from this barren landscape.

One road, narrow and steep, was thickly flanked on either side by sharp thorn bushes and barbed briers, that met overhead and made the pathway a dark tunnel. Another road was broad and fair and full of dancing sunlight, leading over a velvet lawn studded with clusters of jewel-like flowers. The third road wound onward through a ferny brake, moss-grown underfoot and with a green canopy of foliage casting a cool shade overhead.

The Elf Queen followed Thomas' gaze, and told him where the three roads led.

'That steep and narrow road is called the Path of Righteousness,' she said, 'and few travellers are bold enough to take their way along it. The fair, broad road that leads across the lawn is the Path of Wickedness, for all it seems so beautiful and full of light. And the bonny road that winds between the green hedgerow is the path to fair Elfland, where you and I shall be this night.'

She went to her horse, who pawed the ground and tossed his head in eagerness to follow the ferny path; but before they rode on, she said to Thomas:

'If you obey my counsel and remember to keep silence whilst you are in Elfin Land, in spite of all that you may hear and see, then at the end of the seven years that you are bound to serve me you will return to the land of men. But if you speak one word in my domain, you will forfeit your happiness and be doomed to wander for ever the wilderness that lies between fair Elfin Land and the world of men.'

They rode on along the third pathway, and Thomas found that there was still a great distance to traverse before they reached the Queen's domain. They journeyed over valleys and hills, across moor and plain. Sometimes the sky grew black as midnight, and sometimes the sun fringed all the clouds with gold. They forded rushing rivers that ran red blood, when the sides of the milk-white steed were scarlet-splashed and the Queen would kilt up her long green mantle. For all the blood that was ever shed upon the earth ran through the springs of that strange land.

But at last they reached the gates of Elfin Land, where a thousand faery trumpets proclaimed their approach, and they passed through into an enchanted country filled with a splendid light.

And far away, in the land of the earth-born, the men of Ercildourne whispered to one another the weird tale of Thomas Learmont, who had disappeared one summer's day.

. . . . . .

During all the time that Thomas remained in Elfin Land, he spoke no word in spite of all the wonderful things he saw and heard. And when he had served the Elf Queen for seven years, and the time was come for him to take his leave, she herself led him out of the faery gates, into a sunlit garden that lay without. Slender lilies and all fair flowers grew there, and trees adorned with glowing greenness, beneath which gentle unicorns stepped delicately.

The Queen stretched out a hand and plucked an apple from a tree, then held it out for Thomas to take.

' Now at last you may break your silence, Thomas,' she said. ' And take this apple as a reward for the service you have rendered me these seven years. It is an enchanted fruit, and will bestow on you a tongue that can never lie.'

Now Thomas was a quick-witted fellow, and he soon saw that to be unable to speak anything but the truth for the rest of his life might be a doubtful blessing in the world to which he was returning. He tried to explain this to the Queen, saying :

' In the land of men it is often necessary to exaggerate a little if a fair bargain is to be struck with a neighbour; and the favour of women must be won with eloquence.'

But the Queen only smiled and said : ' Hold your peace, Thomas, for my gift to you is not one to be lightly bestowed on any man. Greater than you imagine, it will bring you lasting fame, and cause the name of Thomas Learmont to be remembered so long as Scotland stands.

' Now you must return, Thomas—but first heed my words. A time will come when I shall call you to come back to me, and you must pledge yourself to obey my summons, wherever you may be. I shall send two messengers, whom you will know at once are not of your world. . . .'

Thomas gazed into the black eyes of the Elf Queen, and he knew that the love-spell she had cast upon him seven years since would never lose its power. Gladly he pledged himself to obey her command; and then a sudden drowsiness overcame him. The green garden with its gentle unicorns faded away, and a white mist like falling apple blossom descended from the sky.

.   .   .   .   .

When Thomas awoke, he found himself lying in the leafy shade of the great tree that grew on Huntlie Bank. He started to his feet in bewilderment and stared along the empty pathways of the wood, listening in vain for the music of silver bridle-bells. His seven-year sojourn in Elfland seemed no more than a summer afternoon's dream. He said aloud: ' One day I will return,' and then he picked up his lute and took the way back to Ercildourne, curious to know what had happened there in the space of seven years—and curious, too, about the gift the Elf Queen had laid upon his tongue.

' For I fear I may offend many a neighbour,' he chuckled to himself, ' if I am indeed able to speak nothing but the truth. They will get blunter answers and opinions than they bargain for when they ask my advice about themselves and their doings ! '

As soon as he stepped into the village street a terrified yell went up from a simple old soul who imagined he had sauntered back from the dead. Thomas soon proved himself to be very much alive, however, and before long the good people of Ercildourne got over their surprise at his re-appearance. But they never recovered from their surprise and awe when they heard Thomas' story of his sojourn in Elfin Land. The children would climb on his knee and huddle round his feet, listening eagerly as he told them of the sweet enchantment of that faery world; and the old folk would nod their heads and whisper among themselves of others who had been lured away by the Elf Queen. But one thing that Thomas never spoke of was his pledge to

return to Elfin Land whenever he should be called by the two faery messengers.

For his own part, Thomas was surprised to find that it did not make very much difference whether he was away from Ercildourne for seven days or seven years. True, his cottage was in need of some repair, where the wind had dislodged a few stones in the walls, and the rain had beaten in the thatch on the roof; and true, his neighbours showed a few more wrinkles and one or two more white hairs. But on the whole, through seven springtimes, summers, harvestings, and winter blizzards, everything was much the same.

Each day after his return he waited to discover how the Elf Queen's gift would be fulfilled. He found, to his relief, that he was after all still able to speak fair words to the crofter's daughter, and that he could yet persuade a doubtful neighbour to buy a cow or a sheep.

Then one day, at a gathering of the villagers, when

they were discussing the ravages of a cattle murrain that had befallen the land, Thomas found himself compelled by some mysterious force to get to his feet. Words seemed to fall from his tongue of their own accord, and to his amazement he found himself prophesying that the murrain would not touch a single beast belonging to the neighbourhood of Ercildourne. The villagers were awed by his inspired bearing, and in some strange way they knew beyond a doubt that he spoke the truth—they knew it even before the murrain passed by without harming any of their cattle.

After this, Thomas began to make many prophecies, most of them in rhymes that were easily remembered, and were quoted from mouth to mouth. Again and again they were proved right, and his fame spread throughout Scotland, many rich lords and earls rewarding him for his sayings and marvelling at his uncanny power. But although he visited many parts of the country and met many fine folk, Thomas did not desert Ercildourne. With his new-found wealth he built a fine Tower to live in, and dwelt there for many years. And yet, for all his fame and wealth, men remarked that Thomas was not an entirely happy man. There was always a strange light of longing in his eyes, as though he could not rid himself of the memory of an unearthly world.

Every year Thomas held a grand banquet in his Tower of Ercildourne, to which all the villagers and folk who lived near by were invited. It was a night of gay festivity, when the pipers set feet a-dancing and hearts stirring, and the hall was filled with shouts of revelry. A great feast was provided, with a never-ending supply of frothing ale. And when the dancers rested, and while the ale-stoups were filled once more, Thomas would play his lute.

It was during one such night, while the feasting and gaiety were at their height, that a servant came running into the rush-lit hall with a strange tale on his lips. There was such urgency in his bearing that Thomas rose up in his place and called for silence, so that the servant might make himself heard. The laughter and the shouting died away, and in the sudden quiet the man said:

'Oh, master, I have seen the strangest sight in all the world. A milk-white hart and a milk-white hind from the forest beyond the hill-side are walking down the street outside.'

Strange news indeed! For no beast that dwelt in the forest beyond the hill-side ever ventured beyond those dark trees; besides, who had ever heard of a milk-white hart and a milk-white hind?

The guests, with Thomas at their head, rushed into the street, exclaiming at the sight before them. For sure enough, stepping slowly towards them in the moon-light, undisturbed by the great crowd of people that had suddenly appeared, came the two graceful creatures.

And Thomas knew them to be no earthly creatures, but two faery messengers sent by the Elf Queen to recall him to her service. Happiness overcame him at last as he left the throng and walked slowly away. Then, with the milk-white hart on his right hand and the milk-white hind on his left, Thomas Learmont passed up the village street and went off towards the dark forest, leaving Ercildourne behind for ever.

But, even as the Elf Queen had foretold, Thomas' great gift of prophecy brought him lasting fame, and today you will still hear men quote his saying and repeat his rhymes.

He delivered what was perhaps his most famous prediction on 18 March 1285, when Alexander III, one of Scotland's wisest and greatest kings, was on the throne. On this day, the Earl of March sent for Thomas the

Rhymer, and demanded to know what the next day's weather would be.

'On the morrow, afore noon, shall blow the greatest wind that ever was heard before in Scotland,' Thomas told him.

Late the next morning, the Earl sent for Thomas again.

'Where is this dire wind you spoke of?' he rebuked him, indicating the day's mild weather.

'Noon is not yet gone,' Thomas replied quietly.

Just then, a man burst into the Earl's presence, shouting that the King was dead. He had fallen from his horse on a precipitous cliff path, and had been killed instantly.

'Yon is the wind that shall blow to the great calamity and trouble of Scotland,' said Thomas; and indeed, when the dreadful news was known abroad, universal sorrow for the death of this good king was felt throughout the country, and many years of unrest followed.

Thomas also prophesied:

> *As long as the Thorn Tree stands,*
> *Ercildourne shall keep its lands.*

In the year that the Thorn Tree did fall, all the merchants of Ercildourne became bankrupt, and shortly afterwards the last fragment of its common land was alienated.

And these are two further prophecies which have yet to be fulfilled:

> *When the Cows o' Gowrie come to land,*
> *The Judgement Day is near at hand.*

The Cows of Gowrie are two boulders now lying beyond high-water mark off Ivergowrie, on the Firth of Tay. They are said to approach land at the rate of an inch a year.

> *York was, London is, and Edinburgh shall be*
> *The biggest and bonniest o' the three.*

Lod, the Farmer's Son

THERE was once a farmer who had a son called Lod; and he was a strong, well-set-up lad who knew his own mind. One day his father sent him with a big dish of oat porridge for a party of men who were at work cutting peat-turves; but on the way, Lod spilt the porridge, so that the peat-cutters went without their dinner, and complained to the farmer when they returned that evening. He scolded Lod with a harsh tongue, and told him to leave his house and take twenty-four roads to seek his own way in the world, for he would not keep him longer.

'If that is the way of it,' said Lod, 'I will go now. I only ask that you will give me an iron club with which to protect myself during my wanderings.'

'You shall have that,' said his father, who straightway went to the smithy and made a club in which there was a stone's weight of iron. 'There is a good club for you,' he said.

Lod took hold of the club and broke it with the first shake that he gave it.

'You must make me a proper club that will be strong enough for me,' he said.

18

So back to the smithy went his father, and made another club in which there were two stones' weight of iron.

'Surely this club is strong enough for you,' he said.

But with the second shake that he gave it, Lod broke the club in two pieces.

'Nor is this club strong enough for me,' he said. 'Make me a better one still.'

Into the third club that he forged, the farmer put three stones and a half of iron.

'There cannot be a stronger club in the world,' he said.

At the third shake that Lod gave this new club, it bent almost double.

'It will have to do,' he told his father, putting the club over his knee to straighten it out. 'I have worried you enough with the making of my weapon.'

Then he said farewell and went away from the home of his youth. It was not long before he came to a king's palace, where he thought he might find employment.

'What work can you do?' the King asked him.

'I am a good cow-herd,' answered Lod. 'Herding is the work to which I have always been accustomed.'

'Then it's a lucky day for me that you've come,' said the King, 'for my cattle are disappearing one by one, and I cannot find a herd to look after them properly. Will you take service with me?'

'I will do that if you will pay the wages I ask, which are ten guineas a year, half a boll of meal a week, and as much milk as I shall require for porridge. I take but two meals a day, breakfast and supper. I must have a house to dwell in by myself, a good-sized boiler, and a bed.'

'Well,' said the King, 'these wages are rather high for me to give. Nevertheless, it is no ordinary herd I am wanting, and so I will try you for half a year on these terms.'

Thus Lod took service with the King, and the cattle were given to him to herd. The next day he rose early and set off with them to their pasture, his strong club under his arm. By and by he came to a thicket of thorn-bushes, where he began to gather sticks of fire-wood, while the cattle grazed on the hilly grass-land round about. He was not long in the thicket before the hill-side shook to a mighty tread, and a terrible great giant came before him.

'What are you doing here, little fellow?' roared the giant.

'Och, good sir!' cried Lod, 'do not be frightening me; little is the thing that will frighten me. I am only gathering sticks of fire-wood. If you have come to take the cattle I am herding, do so and leave me alone.'

The giant then went and caught the heaviest and fattest cow of the herd, and tied its four legs together with lengths of heather-rope.

'Come here and help me to hoist this cow on my back,' he called to Lod.

'Och! I am afraid to go near you,' answered Lod.

'Oo! I will not touch you,' said the giant.

So Lod went over to the giant and said: 'You had better put your head in between its legs, and I will go behind you and lift it up on you.'

Now no sooner had the giant followed Lod's crafty advice and put his head in between the cow's legs, than Lod went behind him and felled him with his club. He then released the cow and cut off the giant's head, which he hung all among the green leaves of a tree-branch. Over the giant's body he threw a portion of an old turf dyke to hide him. Nothing further came to trouble him for the rest of that day, and in the evening he returned home with every one of the cattle safe and sound. The

King met him as he came along his homeward way, and said in astonishment:

' You have got all the cattle home safely ? '

' I have; why should I not ? ' said Lod. He did not tell the King what had befallen him during the day, but kept his adventure to himself.

The next day he again rose early and set off for the pasture-land with his cattle. And once again, when he reached the thicket on the hill-side, he went into it to cut sticks for his fire. He had not long been at this when over the crest of the hill came a giant who was even bigger than the mighty one of the previous day.

' What are you doing here, little fellow ? ' he bellowed.

' I am cutting sticks for fire-wood, good sir,' replied Lod. ' Do not be frightening me; little is the thing that will frighten me.'

' Did you happen to see a man like myself here yesterday ? ' asked the giant, frowning. ' For my mother has lost her youngest son.'

' I did not,' said Lod; ' I was not here yesterday. If it's one of my cows you're after, take the biggest and best you can see and go away.'

The giant knocked down the best cow in the herd (which was the same one as his brother had chosen yesterday, so that the poor beast was getting a hard time of it) and tied its legs together with lengths of heather-rope. Then he said to Lod:

' Come here and help me to hoist this beast on my back.'

' Och, no,' said Lod. ' You are frightening me.'

' Oo ! I will not touch you,' said the giant.

Then it all happened as before, that as soon as the giant followed Lod's advice and put his head between the cow's legs, Lod felled him with his big club, cut off his head, and hung it all among the green leaves of the tree-branch.

c

And the body he covered with a portion of the turf dyke, so that no one passing by should discover it.

That night the King again waylaid Lod as he travelled home; and great was his amazement when he saw every one of his cattle as safe and sound as before.

' Surely you have some news for me of how you fared on the hill-side today,' he said.

' I have not.   There is only the heather, the wood, and the peat moss yonder, and they are no news to you,' replied Lod, who still preferred to keep his adventures to himself.

' Well,' said the King, ' you are the good and lucky herd.   I never had a herd that brought all the cattle safely home but yourself.'

On the third day it happened as on the two previous days : no sooner had Lod gone into the thicket on the hill-side than a third giant, even greater than his two brothers, came to steal the best of the cattle.   And him also Lod overcame, so that there were three heads hanging all among the green leaves of the tree-branch, and three bodies lying beneath the turf dyke.

' It cannot be that you have nothing to tell me of the day's happenings tonight,' said the King when he met Lod coming home that evening.

' Why should it not be so ? ' answered Lod.   ' The peaty burn, the mountain ash, and the field of wild mustard are surely unremarkable to you.'

' Now truly you are the best herd in the country,' declared the King, ' and well worth the wages we agreed upon.'

When he rose up the next morning, Lod said to himself: ' I wonder what is in store for me on the hill-side today ?   For surely there cannot be another giant bigger than the three I have already overcome.'

Once again he drove the cattle to their pasture, and

went into the thicket to cut sticks for fire-wood. Before
long a rush of air came over the hill-side that stripped the
leaves from the trees; and it was not the wind that blew
so fiercely, but the breath of a big grey hag who came
striding over to Lod and pointed a scaly, claw-like forefinger at him.

'Here you are, you rogue and rascal, and contemptible
little fellow! You have killed my three fine sons, and
I have come to get my revenge on you.'

Then she went over to him and grasped his sides, and
he gripped her in a wrestler's stance, and the two of them
fell to fighting. Over the soft and rocky ground they
wrestled, bespattered with peat and blood, both of them
locked fast in a deathly struggle. And the old hag was
so strong of sinew that more than once Lod was in fear
for his life, thinking with despair how near he was to his
foe and how far from his friends. But there came a
moment when he made a violent effort and, giving the
giantess a strenuous lift, he broke her legs under her and
her arms above her, and laid her on the flat of her back.

'Now, carline, what is the ransom you will give me if I
deliver you from the pain you are in?' he asked.

'It is great and not little,' she answered weakly. 'It
is a trunk of gold and a trunk of silver that lie under the
threshold of yonder cave.'

'It will be mine,' said Lod. 'And now I will not be
keeping you longer in pain.' And with this he cut off
her head and hung it alongside those of her three sons,
and flung her body by the turf dyke.

That evening the King stopped him on his way and
said:

'Surely some adventure overtook you during your
herding today?'

'The shape of the hills, the green-growing bracken,
and the wheeling of the curlews in the sky were just as

they always have been,' replied Lod. ' I have nothing
of significance to tell you.'

' Och,' said the King, ' you're a marvellous man, and
if only you had been my herd before now, I should have
been spared much trouble in the past.'

On the morrow, for the first time since he began his
herding of the King's cattle, Lod had a peaceful and
undisturbed day; and when he came home in the
evening, he was very much surprised that the King did
not meet him and ask him how he had fared, as usual.
But when he reached the palace, he found everyone within
its gates weeping and wailing on account of the terrible
fate that was about to overtake the King's daughter.

Lod learnt that during the day a big giant with three
heads had descended on the palace from the countryside
round about (for you will understand that the place was
full of giants in those days) and had threatened to kill
everyone within it unless the Princess was delivered up to
him. He had then gone away again, but swore that if the
princess was not brought to his cave that very night, he
would come back to fulfil his threat. With great sorrow
the King had decided that it was his duty to send away
his daughter in order to save his people; and accordingly,
preparations were made for her going. But at the last
moment, the King's squint-eyed, red-haired cook, thinking to get himself a good reward out of this business,
spoke up and undertook to accompany the Princess to
the giant's cave.

' I will kill the giant for you,' he told the King, ' if I
may have the Princess in marriage afterwards.'

The King was not overjoyed at the prospect of having
the squint-eyed, red-haired cook as his son-in-law, but
nevertheless he agreed to this bargain, and so the cook
and the Princess had set off together for the giant's cave a
little while before Lod's return from the hill-side.

Now Lod had loved the Princess from the moment that he had seen her looking out of one of the palace windows on the very first day of his service with the King; and as soon as he heard what terrible danger she was in, he set off at once for the giant's cave. And under his arm he carried the strong iron club that his father had made for him at the third forging.

When he reached the cave, he saw the Princess standing trembling before its black mouth, while the squint-eyed, red-haired cook was hidden safely behind a stone like the great coward he was.

' Ah ! ' said the Princess when she saw Lod. ' Why have you come here ? It is enough that the giant should take me, without your being killed by him.'

' As to that,' said Lod, ' he cannot go beyond his ability, and I have had some experience of dealing with his kind.'

At that moment there was a loud noise from the inside of the cave, and out came the giant himself: a monstrous man clad in skins, with his three ugly heads set on one great neck. When he strode out into the daylight, his eyes were dazzled after the darkness of the cave; and in that instant Lod sprang at him and swept off the three heads; and that was the end of the giant. The force of Lod's blow was so great that he fell down and grazed his arm; and the Princess bound it up with a strip of cloth torn from her dress. She was overcome with joy for her deliverance and love for her deliverer, and proposed that they should return to the palace immediately, so that Lod could claim her for his wife. But he was weary after his day of herding and the long walk he had had to reach the giant's cave; so he told the Princess that he would take a short sleep before they went back, and lay down on the grass and closed his eyes.

Now all this time the squint-eyed, red-haired cook had

kept in hiding behind his stone; but as soon as he saw
that Lod had fallen asleep, out he came, picked up the
giant's three heads, and snatched the Princess by the

wrist.   In vain she struggled to free herself and called
upon Lod, who slept unheeding; and against her will,
she accompanied the cook back to the palace.   There he
displayed the giant's heads before the King, saying that
he had succeeded in saving the Princess, and claimed her
in marriage according to his bargain.   The King agreed
to the marriage, and the wedding-day was fixed.

It was a great wedding-feast, and when all the guests
were assembled, the King looked round about to make
sure that nothing was lacking.   Then suddenly he
frowned.

' Surely there is one missing,' he said. ' Where is my cow-herd ? '

' Here I am,' came a voice from the doorway; and there stood Lod, his gaze fixed terribly on the rascally cook, who turned pale with fear where he sat in the bridegroom's chair.

' O my father, it was this man who delivered me from the giant, and not the cook at all,' said the Princess. ' I knew he would come to save me from this marriage, even as he saved me then.'

' What proof will you give me of that ? ' said the King.

Then the Princess got up from her place and went over to Lod, whose arm was still bound with the strip of cloth torn from her dress.

' This is the wound he received when he took off the giant's heads, and which I bound for him,' she said; and she showed her father the place in her gown where the strip had been torn away.

Then the King saw that what she said was true; and after they had chased the squint-eyed, red-haired cook far from the land, Lod, the farmer's son, and the King's daughter were married with great rejoicing; and if the last day of their wedding was not the best, it was not a whit the worst.

After the festivities were over, Lod took his wife and the King with him to the place where he had herded the cattle, and showed them the heads of the giants and the old grey hag, where they hung on the tree-branch. And at long last the King heard all the tale of the adventures that had befallen Lod during the first days of his hiring.

Then they took away the trunk of gold and the trunk of silver that lay under the threshold of the cave near by, and lived in great wealth for the rest of their days. And if they have not died since, then they are alive still.

The Piper of Keil

IN Kintyre there is a great cave whose black mouth yawns wide among the cliffs of that rocky coast-line. Long ago this cave was the home of the Little People. Men say that beyond its dark opening there are narrow, winding passages that stretch far inland; and somewhere in the midst of all these tortuous pathways was the great hall of the Little People, lit by a thousand faery tapers, and echoing to the music of a thousand faery minstrels. Here they would dance and hold their revels, and wait upon their Queen; and here, too, they would pronounce judgement on any mortal whom they found trespassing in their domain.

But few men dared to venture past the black entrance of the great cave; for the people who dwelt along this Western coast knew well the dangers and enchantments that might befall a mortal man who trespassed on faery ground.

Now at Keil there lived a bold piper named Alasdair, whose playing was famed throughout Kintyre. He would often play his pipes when his neighbours gathered together after the day's work was done, setting their

feet a-dancing to the lilt of a reel, and playing the age-old
airs that his forefathers had piped before him, while the
foaming ale-stoup was passed round for good cheer and
the peat-fire flame, rekindled with a blessing, cast its
warm glow all about.   And always there would be with
Alasdair his little terrier dog, for the two of them were as
fond of each other as a mother and her bairn or a good
wife and her man.

On one such evening, when the merriment was at its
height, Alasdair paused at the end of one of his fine
tunes, and being well cheered by many a draught from
the ale-stoup, he called out to the company:

'Now I'll pipe ye a tune as good as any that's played
by the wee folk themselves in the great cave yonder by
the shore.'

And he took up his pipes again and prepared to play.
But there were many in the company who looked askance
at his words, for it was a bold boast that the piper had
made, and they all of them knew well that the wee folk
were ever jealous of a mortal who strove to equal their
abilities.   And before Alasdair could get more than a
note or two out of his pipes, a certain farmer called Iain
MacGraw spoke up and said:

'Och, Alasdair, ye'd best take back the words ye
have spoken.   It's true enough that ye're the bravest
piper in all Kintyre; but we all of us know that the
wee folk who dwell in yonder great cave can play music
far beyond our own imagining.   It can aye charm a
bairn from its mother's arms, or a man from his true
love's side.'

The piper smiled, and he answered proud and clear:

'Ye've said your say, and I'll take up your words,
Iain MacGraw.   I'll wager ye that I can play my pipes
right through the pathways of yon great cave this very
night and come out again with no harm befallen me;

for there'll be no faery minstrel to challenge my way with sweeter music or a braver tune than this——'

And while the neighbours gasped among themselves at his foolhardy words, Alasdair lifted the pipes to his lips once more and broke into the skirling lilt of ' The Nameless Tune '. And no one among that company had ever heard him play sweeter music or a braver air.

But Alasdair's daring boast had reached the knowledge of the Little Folk themselves, as they held revel in their great hall, and there was anger against the scornful piper of Keil. The thousand faery minstrels pitched their immortal music on a wilder note, and the thousand faery tapers flickered as the Elf Queen herself prepared a strong enchantment to fall upon the bold piper when he should enter her domain. It may be that a foreboding of this enchantment came to the piper's little dog, for the hairs stiffened along his back and he growled low in his throat as Alasdair stepped out from the neighbours' gathering and made his way to the cliff-side, still playing ' The Nameless Tune '. But the dog loved his master too well ever to desert him, and he followed close by his heels as Alasdair approached the black entrance of that great cave.

When they came there, his neighbours stood well aside as the piper strode unfaltering into the darkness, his kilt swinging to his step and his bonnet set jauntily on his head. And by his heels went his faithful little dog. The neighbours strained their eyes to glimpse the last of him as he went away; and long after he had passed beyond their sight they heard the gay, clear music of his pipes. Then there was more than one among the company who shook his head and said:

' I fear we'll never more see our brave piper of Keil.'

It was not long before the gay piping stopped on a sudden with a dreadful squeal. And echoing, echoing

through those twisting passage-ways until it reached the very mouth of that great cave came the noise of eldritch laughter. Then silence. And as the neighbours still stood there, trembling with fear for the fate of their bonny piper, there came limping out of the cave a poor, whimpering little beast with its eyeballs starting out of its head in fright. It had never a hair left on its body; and it was hard to recognize Alasdair's little terrier, who ran far from the cave as though the green faery hounds themselves had been unleashed to chase him.

But there was no sign of Alasdair himself; and though some waited until long after dawn had come across the water, and though they called his name with their hands cupped to their mouths, the piper of Keil was never seen again. And there was not a man in all Kintyre who would venture through the black opening in the cliff-side to seek him; for they had every one heard that eldritch laughter, which no man could remember without feeling a stroking of his spine.

But that is not quite the end of the story of the piper of Keil. One night as Iain MacGraw and his good wife were sitting by the fireside at their farm a few miles inland, the woman suddenly bent her ear to the hearth-stone.

' Do you not hear the sound of the pipes, good man ? ' she asked her husband.

The farmer listened in his turn, and at last he looked up, and there was amazement in his eye. For the sound that they could hear was the playing of ' The Nameless Tune '; and they knew full well that the piper was Alasdair himself, doomed by the Little Folk to wander for ever through the maze of passage-ways that stretched far inland below the ground.

Then, as they listened, the sound of the tune died away and they heard the voice of the piper himself raised in this lament:

'*I doubt, I doubt*
I'll never win out.
Ochone! for my ageless sorrow.'

·   ·   ·   ·   ·

Today men say that still there are folk who have
heard the far-away sound of the piper's playing at the
place where Iain MacGraw's farm once stood; and
always the tune is interspersed with that despairing cry.

The Blue Cap

THERE was once a fisherman of Kintyre called Iain MacRae, who lived at Ardelve. One winter's day, when there was no hope of fishing in the rough sea that had sprung up, Iain decided to build a new keel for his boat, and he came to the woods between Totaig and Glenelg to find a likely length of wood for his purpose.

But he had hardly started to look for his keel when a thick white mist came down from the hills and crept in among the trees. Now Iain had come a fair distance from his home, and as soon as the mist descended his immediate concern was to get back as soon as possible; for he had no desire to become lost and spend a cold winter's night in the open. So he followed a path that he could just discern, thinking it was the one he had come by, and that it would lead him back to Ardelve. But he soon found he was mistaken, for the path came out of the woods into a strange part of the countryside, and when darkness fell he was hopelessly lost on the hill-side. He was just thinking about wrapping himself in his plaid and spending the rest of the night among the

33

heather when he saw a faint light in the distance. He set off towards it eagerly, and as he drew nearer he found that it shone from the window of an old stone shieling such as the crofters used when they took their cattle to the summer pastures.

'Now I may hope for a night's shelter, and a good peat fire to warm myself,' Iain thought; and he clouted heartily on the tumbledown door.

To his surprise there was no reply.

'There must be somebody in there,' he reasoned to himself, 'for a candle does not light itself.'

And he clouted on the door a second time. Still there was no reply, although now he could distinctly hear voices from within the shieling. At this Iain grew angry and shouted:

'What manner of folk are you, that will not allow a weary stranger shelter from a winter's night?'

Then he heard a shuffle of footsteps, and the door was opened just about wide enough to admit a cat, by an old, old woman who peered closely at him.

'I suppose you can stay here for the night,' she said grudgingly, 'for there's no other dwelling within miles. You'd best come in and lie by the hearth-side.'

She opened the door wider, then shut it fast again, and Iain stepped into the little shieling. Burning in the hearth was a bright peat fire, and seated on either side of it he saw two other old crones. The three old women said never a word more to Iain; but the one who had opened the door motioned him to the hearth-side, where he lay down in his plaid. But he did not go to sleep, for he sensed a strange atmosphere in the little shieling, and thought it wiser to keep awake.

By and by, the three old women glanced in his direction, and seeming satisfied that their unwelcome visitor was asleep, one of them got up and went over to a great wooden chest that stood in the far corner. Iain lay quite still and watched as she lifted the massive lid of the chest and drew out a blue cap, which she solemnly placed on her head. Then she cried in a croaking voice:

'Carlisle!'

And to Iain's astonishment she vanished forthwith.

Then, one after the other, the two other old women also went to the chest, took out blue caps, put them on their heads, and cried out: 'Carlisle!' And the instant that they did so, they disappeared altogether.

As soon as the last old crone had vanished, Iain sprang up from the hearth-side and went over to the chest himself. Inside he saw another blue cap exactly the same as the others; and because he was consumed with curiosity as to where in the world the three witches had gone, he clapped it on his head and shouted in a bold voice, exactly as they had done:

'Carlisle!'

All at once the stone walls of that miserable shieling seemed to melt away, and he felt a great whirling and swirling sensation, as though he was being hurled through the air at a reckless speed. Then he was let down with a bump, and when he next looked round, where should he be but in a huge wine-cellar, where the three old crones were merrily drinking among themselves. But as soon as Iain landed in their midst, they left their drinking and started up to their feet, crying:

'Kintail, Kintail, back again!'

And they vanished immediately.

But Iain had no wish to follow them this time, for his present surroundings suited him well. He examined all the casks and bottles carefully, taking a drop here and a draught there, until at last he staggered into a corner and fell into as heavy a sleep as he had ever slept in his whole life.

Now it happened that the wine-cellar to which Iain had been so mysteriously transported belonged to the Bishop of Carlisle, and lay under his Palace in England. In the morning the Bishop's servants came down to the cellar, and were horrified to find a litter of scattered bottles, and to see the wine-casks spilling over on to the floor.

' There have been bottles of wine missing from the racks before now,' declared the Steward, ' but there has never been so shameless a theft as this.'

Then one of the servants caught sight of Iain as he lay in his corner, still deep in sleep, and still wearing his blue cap.

' The thief! the thief!' they all cried; and Iain awoke to find his arms being tied behind his back, and his ankles trussed together like a fowl's.

They brought him as a prisoner before the Lord Bishop, snatching his blue cap from his head; for it was a mark of disrespect for a man to appear in the Palace with his head covered. Then Iain was tried and sentenced to be burnt at the stake for his crime; and a large pile of faggots was heaped round a stout wooden stake in Carlisle market-place. Here Iain was brought and tied to the stake, while a brand was held to the faggots, and the crowd that had gathered to watch the burning waited for the bright flames to spring up.

Now Iain had just about resigned himself to his fate, with a whole lot of heroic thoughts on the edge of his mind, when a sudden idea came to him.

' A last request, a last request!' he cried. ' Let me wear my own blue cap to Eternity!'

His request was granted, and the blue cap was put on his head. Iain no sooner felt it there, than, casting a desperate glance at the flames that were licking the soles of his two feet, he cried out in a bold voice:

' Kintail, Kintail, back again!'

And to the astonishment of the good people of Carlisle, both Iain and the stake he was tied to vanished entirely and were never seen in England again.

When Iain came to his senses once more, he found himself back on the hill-side beyond the woods between Totaig and Glenelg; but of the old shieling where the three crones had lived there was no sign. It was a fine bright day after the night's mist, and Iain saw an old crofter approaching.

'Will you come and release me from this troublesome stake?' he called to the old man.

The crofter came and released Iain as he was bidden.

'But why in the world were you tied to it at all?' he asked.

Iain looked at the stake ruefully: and then he saw that it was a brave piece of wood, stout and serviceable; and he remembered his purpose in setting out from his home in the first place.

'Och, it's a length of wood I've collected to make a new keel for my fishing-boat,' he replied. 'The Bishop of Carlisle gave it to me himself.'

And when the crofter had directed him on to the right road for Ardelve, he set off for home again, whistling cheerfully on his way.

D

How Michael Scot went to Rome

THIS is a tale of Michael Scot, the famous wizard of Selkirk, who was namely for the wonderful deeds he committed beyond men's comprehension; he who split the Eildon Hills in twain.

You will know that in the old days, Scotland was ruled by the Pope from his great palace in Rome; and every year, it was the custom for an intelligent and prudent man to leave the country and travel to Rome for the purpose of finding out from his Holiness the date on which Shrove-tide would fall. This was a very important piece of knowledge for the people to have, because the Feast of Shrove-tide regulated all the other feasts of the Church throughout the following twelve months. On Shrove-tide, Lent began; six weeks after that it was Easter, and so on unto the end of the year.

It happened that one year Michael Scot himself was chosen to go to Rome to obtain this information; but because he had a great many other matters to attend to, he did not remember the duty that had been laid upon him until all the feasts of the year were over at Candlemas.

There was not a moment to lose; and although to any ordinary man the idea of getting to Rome and back in so short a time would have seemed the notion of one out of his senses, to Michael it presented no problem at all. He rose up and betook himself to a green paddock where grazed the magic riding fillies with the white stars on their foreheads and the look of faery in their great golden eyes.

'How swiftly can you ride?' he asked the first filly in the field.

'I am as fleet as the wind,' she replied.

'You will not do,' said Michael.

He went over to the next filly and asked her the same question.

'I am so swift that I can outspeed the wind that comes behind me, and overtake the wind that goes before me,' she told him.

'Nor can you help me,' said Michael.

'I ride faster than the black blast of March,' said the third filly.

'Yet you are not fast enough for me,' said Michael; and he went up to the last filly that was there.

'How swift are you?' he asked her.

'I am as swift as the thought of a maiden between her two lovers,' she replied.

'Then indeed you will be of service to me,' said Michael; and without more ado he mounted her back, and they set off for Rome.

Away they rode with the swiftest speed in the wide world. Sea and land were alike to them, and the filly's shining hooves skimmed the white sea surf as lightly as they passed over the snow-covered hills and the green valleys. Sooner than soon, the misty lands and grey seas were far behind them, and they came into Rome on the wings of a golden morning, and alighted right in front of the Pope's house.

Michael immediately sent message to the Pope that a Scotsman was at the door, and the Pope came at once to the audience-room.

' I am come from thy faithful children of Scotland, seeking the knowledge of Shrove-tide lest Lent will go away,' said Michael.

' You are too late in your coming,' said the Pope, ' for you will never be able to return to Scotland in time with the knowledge, and Lent will indeed pass by.'

' There is plenty of time,' replied Michael, ' for it was but a few moments ago that I left my native land, and I shall return as quickly as I came.'

' A few moments ago ! ' exclaimed the Pope.   ' I'll not believe a word you say.   What proof can you give me of that ? '

Then Michael held out the bonnet that he carried in his hand out of reverence for his Holiness.

' Do you not see the snow on my bonnet ? ' he said. ' That is the snow of Scotland, where the hills are all covered in their winter whiteness.'

' Well, it's a most extraordinary thing,' said the Pope. ' But nevertheless I will tell you what you want to know. The first Tuesday of the first moon of Spring is Shrove-tide.'

When he heard this, Michael was highly delighted, for until now the messenger sent from Scotland each year had obtained but the knowledge that this particular day or that particular day was the day of Shrove-tide in the coming year; and now Michael had learnt the secret of how the Pope himself ascertained Shrove-tide.

' I am greatly obliged to your Holiness,' he said, and took his leave straightway.   Mounting the magic filly again, he accomplished his homeward journey as swiftly as he had come, and made known his news in Scotland.

Tam Lin

FAIR Janet was the daughter of a lowland Earl who lived in a grey castle beside green meadows. One day, tired of sewing in her bower, and tired of playing long games of chess with the ladies of her father's house, she put on a green kirtle, braided her yellow hair, and set off alone to explore the leafy woods of Carterhaugh.

She wandered in the sunlight through quiet, grassy glades full of green shade, where the wild briar roses grew riotously, and white-stemmed bluebells made a carpet for her feet. She stretched out her hand and plucked a pale rose to put at her waist; and no sooner was the flower pulled from the thorn than a young man suddenly stepped into the path before her.

'How dare you pluck the roses of Carterhaugh and wander here without my leave?' he asked Janet.

'I meant no harm,' she answered him.

'I am set to guard these woods, and see that no one disturbs their peace,' said the young man.

Then he smiled slowly, as one who has not smiled for a long time, and pulled a red rose that had grown beside her white one.

' Yet I would willingly give all the roses of Carter-haugh to one so lovely as yourself,' he said.

' Who are you, soft-spoken one ? ' asked Janet, taking his rose.

' My name is Tam Lin,' the young man replied.

' I have heard of you !   You are an elfin knight,' cried Janet; and she cast away the flower in fear.

' There is no cause for fear, fair Janet,' said Tam Lin. ' For though men call me an elfin knight, I was born a mortal child just as you were yourself.'

Then, as Janet listened in wonder, he told her all his story.

' My father and mother died when I was but a bairn,' he said, ' and my grandfather, the Earl of Roxburgh, took me to live with him.   One day when we were hunting in these very woods, a cold, queer wind came from the north and blew through every leaf.   I felt a heavy sleep descend on me; and, lagging far behind my companions, at last I fell from my horse.   And when I woke, I found myself in the faery land, for the Elf Queen had come and stolen me away as I slept.'

Here Tam Lin paused as he thought of that green, enchanted land.

' Ever since then,' he continued, ' I have been bound fast by the spell the Elf Queen put on me.   In the day-time I guard the woods of Carterhaugh, and at night I return to the faery land.   Oh, Janet, there is a great longing upon me to return to the mortal life I left; I wish with all my heart that I could be rid of my enchantment.'

He spoke with such great sorrow that Janet cried out:

' And is there no way this can be achieved ? '

Then Tam Lin caught her hands in his and said:

' Tonight is Hallowe'en, Janet, and on that night of all nights there is a chance to win me back to mortal life.

For on Hallowe'en the faery folk ride abroad, and I ride with them.'

'Tell me what I may do to help you,' said Janet, 'for I would win you back with all my heart.'

'When midnight comes,' Tam Lin told her, 'you must go to the cross-roads, and there await the faery host as it comes riding by. As the first company approaches you, stay still and let them pass; and as the second company draws near, let them pass also. But I shall be among the third company, riding a milk-white steed and wearing a gold circlet on my brow.

'Then run to me, Janet, and pull me from my horse, and throw your arms about me. And no matter what spells they cast upon me, hold me fast and do not let me go. That way will you win me back to earth.'

. . . . .

A little after twelve that night, Janet hastened to the cross-roads, and waited in the shadow of the thorn hedge. The ditches gleamed in the moonlight, the thorn bushes cast strange shapes upon the ground, and the trees rustled their branches eerily above her. And faintly on the wind she heard the sound of bridles ringing, and knew that the faery horses were abroad.

Shivering a little, she drew her cloak about her and peered along the road. First she saw the gleam of silver harness, then the white blaze on the forehead of the horse that came riding first; and soon all the faery host came into sight, their pale, pointed faces upturned to the moonlight, and their curious elfin locks windswept behind them as they rode.

As the first company passed her, with the Elf Queen herself mounted on a black, black steed, she stayed quite still and let them go; nor did she move when the second company went by. But among the third company she saw the milk-white horse that bore Tam Lin, and the glitter of the gold circlet about his brow; and running from the shadow of the thorn hedge she seized his bridle and pulled him to the ground, clasping him in her arms.

At once an eldritch cry rose up:

' Tam Lin is away ! ' and the Elf Queen's black horse reared up as she suddenly pulled him to a halt. She turned, and cast her beautiful, inhuman eyes towards Janet and Tam Lin. And as Janet clasped him in her arms, the Elf Queen's spells fell upon Tam Lin, and he dwindled and shrank in Janet's grasp and became a little scaly lizard, which she clutched to her heart.

Then she felt a slithering through her fingers, and the lizard became a cold, slippery snake which she gripped tight as it coiled about her neck.

All at once a fiery pain ran through her hands, and the cold snake turned into a red-hot block of iron. Tears of pain ran down Janet's cheeks, but still she held Tam Lin fast, and would not let him go.

Then at last the Elf Queen knew that she had lost Tam Lin because of the steadfast love of a mortal woman, and she shaped him in Janet's arms in his own form: a mother-naked man. And Janet cast her green mantle over him in triumph. And as the faery host drew rein once more, and a slim green hand came forth to lead away the milk-white steed Tam Lin had ridden, they heard the voice of the Elf Queen raised in a bitter lament:

' The bonniest knight in all my company is lost to the world of mortals. Farewell, Tam Lin ! Had I but known that an earthly woman would win you with her love, I would have taken out your heart of flesh and put in a heart of stone. And had I known that fair Janet was coming to Carterhaugh, I would have taken out your two grey eyes and put in two of wood.'

As she spoke, a faint dawn light came to the earth, and

with a weird cry the faery riders spurred on their horses and vanished with the night. And as the sound of their bridle bells died far away, Tam Lin caught hold of one of Janet's poor blistered hands, and together they returned to the grey castle where her father lived.

The Secret of Heather-ale

THERE is a legend that long ago the Picts knew the secret of brewing heather-ale; a secret so precious that it was known to only one family, and passed down from father to eldest son. It was jealously guarded during the bitter warfare that troubled Scotland throughout the early years of her history; but during the strife between the Picts and the Scots in the ninth century, it was finally lost for ever.

For at that time Scotland was divided into two Kingdoms: the Kingdom of the Picts, who were the original inhabitants of the land; and the Kingdom of the Scots, who came from Ireland and invaded Alba in the sixth century.

Now the Scots knew well the taste of the legendary ale, and they were determined to learn the secret of its brewing for themselves, so that they might keep the taste upon their tongue for ever. The family that guarded the secret lived in that far western point of Scotland which is known nowadays as the Mull of Galloway; and great was the Scots' rejoicing when the old father and his eldest son were captured by a band of their warriors.

The Scots' leader had the old man and his son brought before him where he rested in the open air, so that he might take their secret from them. All around them grew the heather from which the nectar was distilled; far below the cliff-top the sea broke distantly against the shore, and shrill sea-birds flew overhead. The warriors threatened and cajoled and pleaded with the old man and his son until darkness covered that heather-covered cliff and the sea glimmered in the dusk; but not a word of the secret would either of them impart. Then at last the Scots fell to tormenting their captives to the death; and in his anguish the young man cried out, so that his father knew him to be near the end of his endurance.

Wearily the old man turned his white head to the enemy leader and said:

'I will tell you the thing you want to know. But first put my son to death, that he may not witness the shame I bring upon myself and my people in parting with the secret.'

With a joyful shout the Scot released the captives from their torment; and then he ran his sword through the young man's body.

'It is done, old man. Now tell us the secret of heather-ale.'

But while he and all his band waited in eager expectation, the old man stood still by the body of his son and mocked them with these words:

'Fools! Do you think that either your threats and promises, or all the torments devised by men can ever wrest from me the secret of heather-ale? I heard my son cry out in his distress, and I knew that he could not withstand your torture much longer. For he was young, and to him the thought that he must renounce green grass, the foam-flecked sea, and the race of birds' wings across the sky was unendurable. And so I bade you kill him before he gave away the secret. It has died safely with him. I shall never tell you how to brew heather-ale, do with me what you will ! '

When he heard the old man's words, the Scots' leader tore his beard with rage, and the veins of his forehead bulged with fury.

' Take him ! ' he commanded his men, ' take him and hurl him from the cliff-top. Let him be dashed to pieces on the rocks, and may the sea mourn over him with her salt tears for ever.'

So the old man met his death; and as he fell from that great height, so the secret of heather-ale was lost.

The Legend of Eilean Donan Castle

IN the Highlands and the Hebrides there is an ancient belief that supernatural powers will fall upon a child who, after he has been weaned, is given his first sip from a raven's skull; for the raven is accounted the wisest and most knowing of his kind.

Long ago, there lived a chieftain in Kintail who decided to see for himself whether there was any truth in this belief; and accordingly, he gave his young son Shamus his first drink of cow's milk from the light, fragile skull of such a bird. For a long time there was no sign that the boy possessed any unusual powers. He played and prattled exactly as other children did, and like them he was sometimes wilful, sometimes good.

But one day his father came upon Shamus as he sat under an apple-tree, looking up into the boughs and uttering strange sounds that did not belong to the human tongue. Then, as the chieftain drew nearer to the tree, there was a flap and flutter of wings, and a handful of small birds flew away in alarm.

'Oh, father, you have frightened them away,' said Shamus. 'They were telling me of the warm lands they

49

visit while we are shivering in the winter's cold, and of
the great ocean that lies blue under the sun all day while
the grey waves break upon our shores.'

'But how can that be, my son?' asked the chieftain.
'For the birds do not speak our language.'

'Yet I understand their tongue,' said Shamus, 'and I
can talk to them and listen to their speech as if it were
my own.'

Thus the chieftain discovered that the knowledge of
bird-language had been bestowed upon his son, and he
knew that there was truth indeed in the old belief
concerning the raven's skull.

As the years went by, Shamus' power did not lessen.
When he rode out hunting, he conversed with the falcon
on his wrist; as he walked by the shore, the sea-birds
would tell him of travellers upon the ocean; and the
little birds that flew near his father's house spoke of what
they had seen about the countryside. He grew up to be
a youth blessed with wisdom and courage as well as
supernatural power; and all the clansmen declared him
a worthy heir to follow in his father's place when the
time should come.

But one black day something happened to turn the
old chief's anger against his son and cause Shamus to
leave the land of his birth in sorrow. For while he
was waiting upon his father at the high table one
evening, the chieftain pointed to the smoke-blackened
rafters of the hall, where innumerable birds had made
their nests for as long as anyone could remember, and
said:

'Tell me, my son, what are the starlings chattering
about tonight? I have never known them make so
much noise before.'

Then Shamus lowered his eyes before his father's gaze
and replied:

' If I answer your question, father, I fear you will be angry.'

Naturally, this reply only made his father more curious, and at length Shamus told him:

' The starlings are saying that one day our positions will be changed, and it is you that will be waiting upon myself at your own table in this very hall, father.'

Now as soon as the chieftain heard these words, he was filled with wrath: for what could such a prophecy mean but that one day his son would rise up against him and take his inheritance before it was due to him?

' Traitor ! ' cried the old man, dashing his wine-cup to the floor, ' would you betray your own father? Leave my house, bid farewell to your clansmen, and never let me see you again ! '

And in spite of his protestations of loyalty and devotion to his father, Shamus was forced to say good-bye to his kinsfolk and leave the home he had known all his life. He went forth from Kintail as a poor man, with nothing but the clothes on his back; and when he reached the shore, he thought to himself:

' The whole world lies before me across the ocean. I will find a ship and sail to those blue seas and sun-filled lands of which the birds have spoken.'

Now there happened to be a ship leaving for foreign lands that very day, and Shamus thought himself lucky indeed when he managed to get taken on as one of her crew. Away he sailed, through calm and stormy seas, until the ship came to the fair land of France. Here Shamus decided to continue his journeying on foot, so he set off across the countryside with lightness in his step and his heart ready for adventure.

Before long he came to a great park where lilies grew among the green grass. In the distance he caught a glimpse of gilded turrets against the sky; and then he

knew that he had reached the King's palace. As he
drew near the great gateway, he heard a sound of sawing
and lopping, and saw that an army of wood-cutters was
busy felling a spinney of poplar-trees that stood before
the palace courtyard. But that was not all: to Shamus'
astonishment, he saw that all round the palace the sky
was filled with birds—little brown sparrows whose
shrill cries fell ceaselessly upon the air, so that he had to
cover his ears with his hands.

Just then a servant accosted him and said:

' Ah, stranger, you may well try to shut your ears
against that unholy din, but it will be useless. Not only
outside the palace, but indoors, too, we are assailed with
this incessant chirping and cheeping. It is enough to
drive a man out of his right mind; and the King is at
his wits' end to know how he may rid himself of the
plague.'

At once it occurred to Shamus that he of all men might
be able to help the King in his trouble; and he asked the
servant to take him to his royal master. The servant led
the way through long galleries where hosts of sparrows
beat their wings against the panelled walls; across a
terraced walk where the ladies of the Court vainly tried
to converse with each other above the never-ending
hubbub, and past a room filled with fluted pillars, where
birds perched on every ledge and cornice, drowning the
deliberations of grave counsellors. At last they reached
a little room where the King sat alone. The windows
were shut fast, and a sentry stood guard by the door; but
in spite of these precautions, one sparrow swifter than
his fellows had managed to enter the room when the
Queen visited her lord that morning. The King was
watching the bird where it perched on the arm of his
chair, his chin cupped in one jewelled hand, in an attitude
of deep despair.

' If you please, sire,' said Shamus, ' I think that I of all men may be able to rid you of this feathered curse that has fallen upon your palace.'

At once the King's face brightened and a gleam of hope shone in his eyes.

' If what you say is true,' he declared, ' your reward will be great and you will earn my everlasting gratitude. But why do you imagine that you of all men can help me in my trouble ? '

Then Shamus told the King of his power of speaking with the birds in their own tongue.

' There must be some reason, sire,' he said, ' why the sparrows are waging their shrill warfare against you.' He turned to the little bird that was perched beside the King, and spoke to it in its own language, uttering the strange sounds that his father had first heard him make long ago under the apple-tree. When he had finished speaking, the bird flew on to his outstretched hand and replied with an excited chattering of which the King could not make one word of sense, but which Shamus seemed to understand perfectly. At length he turned to the King and said :

' Why, sire, the solution of your trouble is quite simple. You have incurred the anger of the sparrows because you have ordered the wood-cutters to fell the poplar-trees in which they build their nests, and the birds fear that they will soon be homeless. They promise that if you give orders for the wood-cutters to stop their work, then they will trouble you no more.'

At these words the King rose up and flung wide the door of his room, issuing commands to his sentry. Forthwith six heralds with six silver trumpets went out to proclaim that not another tree, bush, branch, or twig that stood within the palace grounds should be lopped off. And again he swore by his bushy beard and by all

E

the Saints of France that if after this the birds plagued
him no more, then Shamus would be richly rewarded.

No sooner had the last wood-cutter's axe fallen silent,
than from the long, panelled galleries, from the terraced
walk where the ladies sat, from the pillared room where
the counsellors deliberated, and from every nook and
cranny throughout the palace, a great company of sparrows
flew out and soared away above the gilded turrets, to
rebuild their nests among the poplar-trees.   And from
that day the King of France was never troubled by so
much as one little sparrow as long as he lived.

True to his word, he rewarded Shamus richly for his
help, giving him a long galley fully equipped and
manned, and a quantity of gold.

In this fine new ship Shamus sailed away across the
water to seek more adventure.   He visited the lands of
dark-skinned peoples, where gold lies unheeded upon the
ground, like so many pebbles on the hill-side; and he
sailed between fair islands where no man's foot had ever
left its imprint.   And wherever he went he gained
wealth and wisdom.   But in all these distant places
Shamus never forgot the hills, the mountain tarns, and
heather slopes of Kintail, and after ten years of roaming
he could no longer withstand his great desire to return
home and see his own people once more.

On a day of days his rich galley with its golden prow
nosed its way through the creeks of the misty Hebridean
sea, and anchored in the narrow channel between Totaig
and a certain rocky islet.   When they beheld the great
ship there, Shamus' kinsfolk and clansmen gasped at its
magnificence and wondered what rich stranger had come
to their shore.   They took the news to the old chieftain
himself—he who had sent forth his son so long ago—
and he came out to welcome the stranger and offer him
hospitality.   He did not recognize his son in the hand-

some man who accepted the shelter of his roof, but treated Shamus with all the honour due to a young nobleman of courteous bearing.

But that evening, during the great feast that had been prepared for him, Shamus disclosed his identity and healed the unhappy rift between himself and his father. For, following the custom of those days, which decreed that the master of a house should himself wait upon an honoured guest, the old chieftain brought wine to Shamus as he sat at the high table; and as the old man knelt before his son, bearing the drinking-cup, Shamus cried:

' Oh, my father, do you not remember me? I am your son whom you sent away in wrath because of the prophecy of the birds. Now that prophecy has come true: for you are waiting upon me at your own table. Oh, father, receive me as your son again. Once more I swear to you that the thought of treachery was never in my heart, nor did I ever harbour any evil design against you.'

At these words the old man sprang up with a glad shout, and fell on Shamus' neck. In the sight of all the company assembled in the hall he restored his son to his inheritance; and great was the clansmen's rejoicing.

When the tale of Shamus' wanderings was told, his fame as a traveller spread far and wide, until at last it reached the ears of the King of Scotland himself. Now at that time the western coast was much harried by the Norsemen's attacks, and the King wished to find a man of trust whom he could place in command of a stronghold off Kintail. He summoned Shamus to his Court, and finding him a man of great wisdom, he commanded him to build a castle on Eilean Donan, that rocky islet opposite Totaig, to be a watch-post and a stronghold against the Norse invaders.

Black Colin of Loch Awe

ONE of the most powerful clans in Scotland is the Clan Campbell. For many centuries the home of the chiefs of Clan Campbell, Barons of Lochlow, was in Glenurchy, on an islet at the head of Loch Awe, whose still waters reflect the slopes of Ben Cruachan: the mountain which gave the Campbells their battle cry, '*Cruachan!*'

Here, some five hundred years ago, a son was born to the chief and was given the name Colin. Following the Highland custom of those days, the child was sent away from his father's house and entrusted to the care of a farmer's family, to spend his boyhood among the humble clansmen whose chief he would become one day. Colin loved his foster-family well, and grew up full of strength and courage. No other youth could excel the young chief in wrestling, hunting, or swimming, and none showed such skill as he with the dirk and the claymore. Colin won for himself a loyal following among his clansmen, to whom he became known as 'Black Colin', on account of his swarthy appearance and stern prowess in fighting. For those were lawless days, when each clan had to protect its territory and fortunes from marauding neighbours by strength of arms, and the young chief took part in many a skirmish. There was one neighbour baron who looked on the Campbell lands and possessions with especial covetousness, and his name was Neil MacCorquodale.

In time the old chief died, and Colin took on the leadership of his clan, becoming Lord of Glenurchy and taking a fair wife to dwell with him as his lady. Yet in spite of the devotion of his clansmen, his prosperity and power, and the happiness of his marriage, in his heart Black Colin was restless. He was tired of the unimportant warfare and petty skirmishes with his neighbours; he longed to set out upon a great enterprise which would test his valour to the full and satisfy his desire to bring greater glory to Clan Campbell.

And then, one summer day, there came to his castle a stranger who brought the very opportunity he was seeking. The stranger was a humble man who made his way to Glenurchy on foot, leaning upon a heavy staff. He was a Palmer, returning to the home whence he had set out many years ago to visit the holy shrines in the Kingdom of Jerusalem. He brought bad news of the Holy Land, for the Infidels stormed the holy places and waged ceaseless battle against the pilgrims and the Christian faith. The Pope had called for a new Crusade to fight for the Holy Cross, and had promised that his blessing would be upon the man who set out against the Infidel.

As soon as Black Colin learnt of this, he was filled with an unquenchable desire to take part in the Crusade, and he swore upon the hilt of his dirk that he would go forth to defend the faith and receive the Pope's blessing on behalf of his clansmen. In vain his young wife besought him to renounce his vow, for the lands of Jerusalem were immeasurably far away, and who could say whether Black Colin would ever return to Glenurchy? But his resolution was firm, and he told his wife that she should take his place over the clansmen while he was gone, holding the islet castle in his stead.

'Wait seven years for my return,' Black Colin said, 'and then if I have not come back, for your consolation and happiness take another husband to rule Glenurchy with you.'

'I will wait seven times seven years,' replied his lady, 'but I can never love another husband as I love you. Yet let there be some token between us that you will send me from your death-bed, so that I shall know for sure whether you are alive or not, and shall not live with a vain hope in my breast.'

Then Black Colin ordered a gold ring to be made, and on the inner side he had both their names engraved. This token he broke in two pieces, giving the half bearing his name to his lady, and keeping the other half himself.

'I will part with this only when I am dying,' he said, 'and it shall be the token whereby you shall know that I will never return to you.'

Then, with a few faithful clansmen, Black Colin left Glenurchy for the Holy Land, taking ship at Leith and travelling across the Alps to Rome. Here he obtained audience of the Pope, who sent him to join the Knights of St John at Rhodes.

Far indeed from the mists and sombre landscape of Argyll was this sun-filled island of olive-trees and crimson roses, surrounded by a brilliant sea. The Knight Templars' fortress stood white and impregnable, looking towards the low-lying Turkish coast, and the soldiers of God with the white cross emblazoned on their red

tunics fought valiantly for His glory. Black Colin
gained great honour in battle, and remained at Rhodes
for several years, the only survivor of his faithful band
of clansmen. Yet still he felt that his soul's ambition
was unfulfilled, and when he left Rhodes he decided to
make a pilgrimage to the holy shrines before he returned
home.

And while he passed by the Sea of Galilee and
journeyed to the Mount of Olives and Golgotha, and
while he adored the Holy Sepulchre, the seven years of
the covenant he had made with his wife were fulfilled.
But although he always carried the gold token on his
heart, Black Colin did not realize that the time of his
return had slipped by, and still he stayed far from home,
while in Glenurchy the clansmen mourned their chief
as though he were dead.

But the Lady of Glenurchy believed that her lord yet
lived, for she had received no token from his death-bed.
Many suitors came to woo her in marriage, saying that
Black Colin had surely died fighting for the Holy Cross,
and that no woman should wait longer than seven years
for her husband's return; but to each one she replied
that until she received the death-bed token from her
lord, she would never marry again. This answer
defeated all her suitors save one, and that was Neil
MacCorquodale, who sought to bring about a powerful
alliance with his neighbour barony by marrying the
widow of his old enemy.

Determined to win her, the Baron conceived a cunning
plan whereby he would convince the lady that her
husband was indeed dead. His first thought was to
have sent to her a copy of Black Colin's token by a
messenger who would swear that her lord had given it
to him as he lay dying; but when she steadfastly refused
to disclose the nature of the token, he resorted to another

stratagem. He came before her one day with a travel-worn companion who said that he had come straight from Rome with a letter for the Lady of Glenurchy; and when she opened it, she found that it contained the news that Black Colin had been killed in Rhodes.

At last she raised her eyes and said:

'Have you nothing else for me besides this letter? Do you not carry a token for me?'

'There is no token, lady,' replied the Baron's companion. 'But I have another message to deliver which I received in Rome from the last survivor of that Campbell following which went with your lord across the sea. He told me that as your lord lay dying, he entrusted him with a last message and a precious token to deliver to you. The message was that you should remember your lord's desire for you to wed again, and take another husband to rule Glenurchy with you.

'But what the token was, I cannot say, for shortly afterwards it was taken by the Saracens in their pillaging, when its bearer was himself so grievously wounded that he has lain sick in Rome for many months.'

Then the Baron and his companion rode away, and a terrible grief overcame the Lady of Glenurchy on account of this false story. She remembered that Black Colin had indeed exhorted her to marry again if he should not return, and she saw that an alliance between herself and Baron MacCorquodale would ensure the future welfare and safety of her clan. And so, because it was better to have so powerful a neighbour as a friend rather than an enemy, she at last consented to marry him.

Yet in spite of all, some strange hope still lingered that her lord yet lived, and because of this she was determined to delay the marriage as long as possible. She told the Baron that their wedding should not take place until she had finished building a new castle on Innis Eilean, in

memory of her husband, and to command the head of
Glenurchy and Loch Awe. As soon as the last stone of
this castle was set in its place, the days of her mourning
would be over and she would become his wife.

Unknown to the Baron, she told the builders to work
as slowly as possible; but in spite of this, the walls of
the castle grew gradually higher, and still there was no
news of Black Colin.

Now in Glenurchy there was another woman who
believed that her chief still lived; and this was Colin's
old foster-mother, who distrusted Baron MacCorquodale
and hated to think of him usurping the place of her
rightful lord. She summoned Iain, her eldest son, and
told him to make his way to Rome, where he must try
by every means to discover what had really happened to
Black Colin. And Iain, who would willingly have died
for the sake of his beloved foster-brother, set off with his
mother's blessing on his head. He journeyed across the
sea and across the land until he reached the splendid city
whence men set out to succour the Holy Cross. And
there, after many days of searching, in a little street of
sunlight, he came face to face with Black Colin, who had
lately come back to Rome from the Holy Land.

Black Colin seized his foster-brother by the arm and
greeted him with incredulous joy.

' Is it really you ? ' he exclaimed. ' What can your
business be in Rome ? '

Then, without more delay, Iain told his chief how all his
people mourned him as one dead, and how his wife,
albeit against her will, was preparing to marry Neil
MacCorquodale, who had brought false evidence of
Colin's death.

' And yet I think she still believes you are alive, and
seeks to delay the marriage as long as she can,' Iain
concluded.

When Black Colin heard this news, he bitterly reviled himself for procrastinating his return.

' It is as though I had tasted of the lotus flower,' he said.   Then he demanded urgently: ' Is there yet time for me to return before my lady contracts this marriage ? We must surely set off at once.'

And together they went immediately and found a ship that would carry them back across the seas.

Had that ship crossed the ocean with the speed of the swiftest bird in the sky, still it would have been too slow for Colin; but at last she anchored off the Scottish coast, and on a day of days the chief and his foster-brother came over the hills into Glenurchy.   Then Colin sent Iain ahead to find out what had happened while he was away, and told him to bring back with him a suit of ragged clothing, such as a beggar might wear.

On his return Iain reported that the wedding between the Baron and the Lady of Glenurchy was to take place the very next day, for the last stone of the fine new castle on Innis Eilean had been set in position, and there was nothing to delay the marriage further.

' Nothing save my return ! ' said Colin.   ' Now listen carefully.   You must go on to your mother's house and wait for me there.   I shall put on these ragged garments and follow you; but on no account must you give any sign that you know me when I first enter your mother's house.'

Iain accordingly set out for his mother's cottage, and the joyful greeting he met with on his return was barely begun when there was a knock on the door, and there stood Black Colin in his beggar's disguise.   The shelter he asked was willingly granted him by his good-hearted foster-mother, who invited him to share a meal with herself and her son.

Now as she went to stir the broth that simmered in a

great cauldron over the fire, Colin saw tears falling down
the old woman's wrinkled cheeks, and he said:

'What is the matter, good woman? As I came in I
heard you greeting your son with joy; but now you are
heavy with sadness.'

'So it is, stranger,' she replied. 'I am glad that my
son is returned from a long journey, yet I am sorrowful
that he has returned alone. For he went forth to seek
one who has been gone from us for many years; and now
I fear that the one he sought is indeed dead.'

Then Colin sprang up and embraced her.

'Not dead, my clanswoman, not dead!' he cried.
'For here I am before you, returned to my own place
and my own people.'

The old woman's joy was splendid to see, but Colin
interrupted her expressions of amazement and continued:

'You must help me, mother, in this matter of the
marriage between my lady and Neil MacCorquodale.
I do not wish to reveal myself until I have discovered
whether I still hold my lady's heart. For the law says
that if a man is away for longer than seven years, then his
wife is free to marry again; and I have no right to claim
my lady unless she still loves me.'

The old woman thought for a space of time, and then
she said:

'Here is the thing that you must do, my son. . . .'
And forthwith she described a plan that pleased Colin's
heart greatly, so that he agreed to follow her counsel.

The next day, still clad in his beggar's garments, he
rose up and went to the great door of his own house,
where the wedding-feast was being held. There was a
huge gathering within the hall of the house, and a spirit
of rejoicing was upon all the people save one: and that
was the Lady of Glenurchy herself, who sat pale and
cheerless in the splendid wedding-gown. There were

many other beggars clustered round the great doorway besides Colin, for generosity and a wedding-feast go hand in hand, and they hoped to obtain many favours.

Yet although the other beggars were content to accept their meat and drink from the servants of the household, Black Colin refused the platter and horn when they offered it to him and declared:

'I will accept no favour unless it is given to me by the hand of the bride herself.'

The servants scoffed at his words, and warned him that the Lady of Glenurchy would be displeased at his bold request. But when she heard of it, the bride rose up from her place and went to the doorway to take a platter of meat and a horn of ale to the beggar-man according to his wish.

'For who can tell?' she said, when the proud Baron MacCorquodale rebuked her for her action, 'in spite of all, Black Colin himself may be wandering abroad in such distress as this beggar at my door, and I would not have it that any one should ignore his need as you advise me to ignore this poor fellow's.'

Black Colin ate the meat from the platter she held out to him, and drank the ale she offered. But when he handed back the horn, he placed inside it the token that he had promised to send her when he lay dying: the half-ring engraved with her name. And as he did so, he raised his eyes and gazed upon her face. By this act she might know that although he was indeed alive, she was not bound to acknowledge him as her husband unless she so desired.

As soon as she encountered Black Colin's gaze, even before she picked up the gold token from the drinking-horn, the lady knew that her husband stood before her, and her heart leapt in unimagined happiness as she stepped forward to embrace him. Then Black Colin knew that his lady's heart belonged to him still, and joyful indeed was their reunion.

Joyful, too, were the clansmen when they knew their chief had returned at last; and all that day and night there were celebrations throughout Glenurchy, and the wedding-feast was turned into a banquet for a hero's homecoming.

As for the false Baron, he fled away in mortal terror, for now his deception of the Lady of Glenurchy was discovered, and he feared Black Colin's vengeance. But the lady intervened on his behalf, and though he little deserved it, his safety was assured.

And to the fine house on Innis Eilean that his lady had built while he was away, Black Colin gave the name of Kilchurn Castle, which it bears to this day.

The Faery Flag of Dunvegan

FOR over a thousand years, Dunvegan Castle, which stands in the west of Skye, has been the home of the MacLeods of MacLeod. Across the waters of Loch Dunvegan, many chieftains have gone forth in times now passed to lead the clansmen against their hereditary enemies, the MacDonalds of Eigg, who were long known as the lawless Lords of the Isles. And perhaps the most treasured possession of the Clan MacLeod is the Faery Flag, which has been passed on from generation to generation until the story of its origin has become a famous legend.

In far distant ages there was once a chief of the Clan MacLeod who was called Malcolm. On a day when the waters of Loch Dunvegan reflected a summer sky, and the heather splashed its glorious purple over the hills, he took a fair lady of the faery folk to be his bride; and for a little while he and his faery wife dwelt peacefully together in the grey Castle of Dunvegan. But the faery folk could never find perfect happiness in the land of men; and when she had borne a fine son to her lord, Malcolm's fair lady felt a great longing to rejoin her own people;

a longing far stronger than the love she had for her mortal husband. And because he could not bear to see his beloved wife unhappy, Malcolm said that he would himself escort her upon the path that led back to her own country. So it happened that this faery woman took fond leave of her tiny child as he lay in his cradle, and went with her husband across the Loch to take the road that would lead her home once more.

And although it was just such a bright summer's day as that on which he had first brought her to the castle as his bride, yet it seemed to Malcolm that the waters of the Loch were dark and dowly, so heavy was the grief that lay upon him. When they came to the far shore, he carried his lady from the boat in his arms, and gently set her upon the ground. Then he accompanied her a little upon her way; but when they reached the span of grey stones that was known as the Faery Bridge, she bade him come no farther, and went on her path alone. Never a backward look she gave; and Malcolm saw his fair wife no more.

Now that very night a great feast was held in the hall of the castle, to celebrate the birth of Malcolm's son, who would one day succeed his noble father as Chief of the Clan MacLeod. And heavy-hearted as he was, Malcolm had perforce to join in the rejoicing and revelry, for this feast was held by ancient tradition. Besides, he himself felt a great pride in his child, destined to be the future MacLeod of MacLeod.

Many clansmen filled the great hall, which blazed with the light of a hundred torches; and the castle servants ran to and fro bearing platters heaped high with succulent venison and flasks full of the good golden ale. And throughout the night the brave pibroch sounded as the men of the Clan MacCrimmon, hereditary pipers to the Clan MacLeod, played stirring music for Malcolm's guests.

In a turret far removed from the noisy gathering in the great hall, the babe who was the cause of all this rejoicing lay quietly asleep in his cradle. His nurse sat beside him as he slept, imagining to herself the cheerful company and the good cheer that would be filling the hall. She was but a girl, young and comely; and as the moon rose high and shone into the solitary turret, a great desire came upon her to take just one peep at the gay revelry. She glanced at the sleeping child; and it seemed that he lay quiet and tranquil enough. So she rose softly to her feet and tiptoed across the rush-strewn floor. Then she fled swiftly along the twisting, moonlit passage-ways and down the winding steps until the skirl of the pipes beat full upon her ears and she came into the great hall. For a while she sat at the far end of the hall, intent on the gaiety and merriment all around her; and when she had feasted her eyes enough, she got up again and prepared to go back to the turret. But as she rose to go, a sudden fear set her heart lurching. For Malcolm himself rose up from his place at the high table and looked in her direction.

' Oh, black the moment that ever I thought to leave the bairn alone,' she thought, ' for the anger of MacLeod will surely be raised against me.'

But although Malcolm had indeed fixed his gaze on her, it did not occur to him that she had done wrong in joining the feasting; for he supposed that she would have left the child in the care of some other servant while she was away from his side. So he called out to her in a voice that had no anger in it, and commanded her to fetch his son before all the company, that he might show the clansmen their future chief.

Trembling with relief, the nurse slipped away to do his bidding, hoping earnestly in her heart that no harm had come to the child in her absence.

Now after the babe had been left alone in the turret, he had slept on for a while in peace. But soon an owl flew past outside with a weird screech, and this disturbed the child, so that he woke in fright. When no one came to comfort him and rock him to sleep again, he started crying; and the sound echoed forlornly through the deserted room.

But though no human ears heard his crying, in a manner unknown to men it reached the hearing of his faery mother as she dwelt in the midst of her own Fair Folk. And dear as her earth-born child was to her heart, by eldritch means she hastened to be beside him and comfort him when no one else was near. She might not take him in her arms; but instead she spread over him a shining faery covering of grass-green silk, embroidered with elf spots and wrought with unearthly skill. As soon as the child felt this faery covering, which brought the comfort of a mother's embrace, he stopped his crying and smiled a little as he settled down to sleep again. And seeing her babe so peaceful and serene, his mother went from his side.

When the child's anxious nurse came back to the turret, she was thankful beyond speech to see how peaceful her young charge lay. But when she saw the covering that lay over him, she was aware that faery folk had been beside him; for she knew the faeries' own green hue, and she recognized the elf spots embroidered on the silk. Yet the bairn himself had taken no harm; and as she sent up a prayer of thankfulness that it was not some changeling child she had discovered lying there, she vowed never again to leave him alone.

Then she took the child in her arms, still wrapped in his faery covering, and bore him to the great hall, according to MacLeod's command. As she neared the feasting and revelry, a sound of enchanted music swept along the

F

passage-ways behind her.   It filled the air and hovered
over the child in her arms, drowning the sound of the
MacCrimmons' pipes, whose pibroch died away as
everyone in the great hall fell silent in amazement.   And
as MacLeod and all his clansmen sat listening, they heard
the sweet voices of a faery host chanting the legend that
was to be remembered as long as there was a man living
to bear the name MacLeod.

They sang that the child's green covering was a faery
flag, the gift of the Little People to the Clan MacLeod,
to remain in their possession so long as that great name
was known in Scotland.   And they foretold that the
waving of the flag would save the Clan in the midst of
three great dangers; but that on no account was it ever
to be waved for a trivial reason.

Then, as Malcolm and the clansmen listened, motion-
less, and the nurse still clasped the babe in her arms, the
faery voices changed.   On a lower and more sombre
note they prophesied the curse that would fall upon the
Clan MacLeod if ever they disregarded the true value of
their faery gift, and waved the flag at a time other than
that of dire necessity.

For then it would come to pass that three dreadful
events would follow the waving of the flag, in whatever
age of century it might take place.   The heir to MacLeod
of MacLeod would shortly die; the group of rocks at
Dunvegan which were called the Three Maidens would
fall into the hands of a Campbell; and at a time when a
red fox brought forth her young in a turret of the castle,
the glory of the MacLeods would depart, they would lose
a great part of their lands, and there would not be sufficient men left in the Chief's own family to row a boat over
Loch Dunvegan.

The Little People had bequeathed their gift and pro-
nounced the curse that attended it; and their voices

died away as a mist dissolves on the hill-side, until there was not a wisp nor a whisper left.

Then Malcolm rose from his place, and took the faery flag from about his son. Carefully he smoothed its green folds and gave instructions that it should be placed in an iron casket of fine workmanship, that would henceforth be borne at the head of the clansmen whenever they went to do battle. And he decreed that none but MacLeod of MacLeod himself should ever take out the flag, to unfurl it and wave it aloft.

.   .   .   .   .

In time, Malcolm departed from this earth, and his son after him. And generations passed by, with the faery flag still safely in the keeping of the clan, until there came a day when the MacDonalds came in great force against the MacLeods. For the old enmity of the two clans still raged fiercely, although there was many a marriage between a MacLeod and a MacDonald. Indeed, it is said of them that they were constantly putting rings on each other's fingers, and dirks into each other's hearts. On this occasion the MacDonalds were determined to humble the pride of the MacLeods for ever, and after landing at Waternish, they advanced to Trumpan and sacked the church there.

Meanwhile, the Chief of MacLeod had rowed across Loch Dunvegan to lead his clansmen against the Mac-Donalds; and at Trumpan a battle took place that raged long and hotly. At length, however, it was clear that the MacLeods, hard-pressed, were being forced to give ground to the MacDonalds; and it was obvious that to overcome the invaders they must rely on a strength other than that of the claymore and the dirk.

It was then that the Chief of MacLeod called for the iron casket that held the faery flag. He undid the clasps and lifted out the frail square of green silk, thinking to himself that surely it was for no trivial reason he now called on the faery power. In the midst of the battle the flag was held aloft in the sight of all the clansmen, who watched in awe as it unfurled and waved above them.

Immediately, there was a change in the fortune of the fight, for it seemed to the MacDonalds that the MacLeod forces had suddenly become reinforced, and were swelled in strength. Thinking themselves outnumbered, they faltered and fell back, and the MacLeods pressed home their advantage and carried the day in triumph. This was the first occasion on which the power of the faery flag was invoked and proven.

The cause of the second unfurling of the flag was of a different nature. Once again the fortunes of the clan were threatened; but not by an enemy who wielded a claymore or hurled a dirk. A plague fell upon their cattle, until there was scarcely a beast left that was untouched by the murrain. The clansmen were overcome with great hardship, for upon their cattle depended the greater part of their livelihood and welfare. When the Chief of MacLeod saw the distress that had fallen on his people, and realized how few beasts were left in the pastures, he knew that if the prosperity of the clan were to be restored, he must call on a power beyond human strength. So he brought forth the faery flag from its iron casket, and he said, as his ancestor had said before him :

'Now surely it is for no trivial reason that I call on the faery power.'

Then the flag was raised aloft, and it unfurled and waved over the stricken land. From that moment, not another beast was touched by the plague, and many on whom the murrain had already descended, recovered. And this was the second occasion on which the power of the faery flag was invoked and proven.

Time passed, and the faery flag was handed from Chief to Chief as the generations went by. In the year 1799 a man called Buchanan was employed as factor to MacLeod of MacLeod. Now like everyone else, he had learnt the legend of the faery flag, and knew also of the curse—as yet unfulfilled—that attended it. But he was a sceptical man, and scorned to put his belief in any superstitious fancy. He declared that the flag was no more than a square of rotting silk, and the legend merely a tale that old wives whispered to each other.

One day, at a time when the MacLeod himself was away from Dunvegan, Buchanan decided to test the curse for himself, and explode once for all the superstitions that hung about the flag. There was an English blacksmith in the village; and it was he whom Buchanan employed to force open the iron casket containing the flag; for the key to the casket was always in the possession of the Chief. When the lid was up, he took out the frail green square and waved it in the air. And surely no man could have thought of a more trivial reason for invoking the faery power.

To those who had never doubted the strength of the faery curse, the events that followed appeared inevitable. In a short while, the heir to MacLeod was blown up in H.M.S. *Charlotte*, and the Maidens were sold to Angus Campbell of Esnay. And it came to pass, exactly as the faery voices had foretold so long ago, that a tame fox belonging to a Lieutenant Maclean, who was staying in Dunvegan Castle, brought forth her young in the west turret; and at this time the MacLeod fortunes began to decline, and a great part of their estates was sold. Although the prosperity of the clan was gradually retrieved, much of its glory vanished for ever; and there was a time not long distant when there were only three MacLeods left in the Chief's own family: not

sufficient to row a four-oared boat over Loch Dunvegan.

Today the faery flag remains in a glass case in Dunvegan Castle; and all who know its strange history stop
to wonder at this threadbare piece of ancient silk, brown
with age, on which the embroidered elf spots may still
be discerned.

Whippety Stourie

O N a day long ago, when the bracken sprang green and tender on the hills, a fine gentleman rode over the braeside to woo a fair lady. As the summer passed the lady came to love her suitor very dearly; and by the time that the bracken hung crisp and golden on the hills they were married with great rejoicing, and he took her away from her father's home to live in his own house.

The lady thought she had never been happier in all her life, for she had all that her heart desired: a great house, rich velvet gowns, and beautiful jewels. But one day her husband came to her and said:

'Now, wife, it is time you put your fair hand to the spinning-wheel; for a home is no home without the clack of a shuttle within its walls; and a wife is no wife unless she can spin fine thread for her husband's shirts.'

The lady looked downcast at these words, and she displayed her hands imploringly.

'Alas,' she said, 'I have never spun a single thread in all my life, husband, for in my father's house it was not thought fitting that a maid of high degree should learn such a lowly occupation.'

75

Then her husband's face grew dark and he replied:

' To sit by the spinning-wheel and spin fine thread is a womanly task that all good wives should perform. From now on you must spin me twelve hanks of thread each day—or, dear as you are to my heart, it will be the worse for you.'

' Truly, husband,' his lady wept, ' I am not too proud to do your bidding, for I would willingly obey your slightest wish. But I fear I shall never be able to spin one good hank of thread, let alone twelve. For how shall I set about my spinning, with no one to show me the way it should be done ? '

But her husband would not listen to her pleading, and only replied that she must find out for herself how to spin. Then he ordered the servants to bring a spinning-wheel to his lady's room, and to provide her each day with sufficient flax to spin twelve hanks of thread.

During the week that followed, the lady rose early each morning and sat herself down before the spinning-wheel, with a heap of shining flax by her side. But though she turned the wheel from the time the sunlight first struck the heather on the hills until it grew dusk, she did not spin one good hank of thread. Every night when her husband came to her room, he would find her resting wearily on her stool and weeping bitterly. Then he would pick up the shuttle and see perhaps half a hank of ravelled and knotted thread.

' This is not the fine thread I want,' he said, ' but coarse stuff, fit for a crofter's garments. You must do better than this, wife—or, dear as you are to my heart, it will be the worse for you.'

On the last night of the week he came to her and announced that he was going away on a journey.

' And when I come back,' he said, ' you must have spun a hundred hanks of fine thread. If you have not, then,

dear as you are to my heart, I must surely cast you aside
and find a new wife to spin for me.'

(For you must know that in those days if a man was not
satisfied with his first wife, he could cast her aside just so
and get himself another instead.)

And he kissed his wife farewell and rode away.

' Alas, alas,' the lady grieved, ' what shall I do now ?
For I well know that I shall never manage to spin a
hundred hanks of fine thread before my husband returns ;
and he will surely cast me aside and find a new wife.'

She left her room and went out to the braeside to
wander among the bracken and the heather, full of
sorrowful thoughts. She had not gone far when she
felt weary, and sat down on a flat grey stone in the shade
of a scarlet-berried rowan-tree. By and by she heard a
faint sound of music; and to her amazement it seemed to
be coming from underneath the very stone where she
sat.

' Now surely it is faery music I can hear,' she thought.
' For I never heard a mortal piper play such a bonny
tune.'

And plucking a twig of the rowan-tree to protect
herself, she jumped up and rolled away the stone, to find
that it had concealed the entrance to a green cave in the
hill-side. Peering inside the cave, she was surprised to
see six wee ladies in green gowns, all sitting round in a
circle. One of them had a little spinning-wheel before
her, and as the shuttle clacked busily to and fro she
sang:

> ' *Little kens my dame at hame*
> *That Whippety Stourie is my name.*'

Without taking a second thought, the lady stepped into
the cave and greeted the Little Folk pleasantly. They
nodded to her in reply; and she noticed that all their six
mouths were as lop-sided as a fir-tree leaning against the

wind. Now as soon as she saw the fine, fine thread
that the wee lady called Whippety Stourie was spinning,
the lady was reminded of all her troubles, and she could
not stop the tears from trickling down her cheeks.

' Why do you weep ? ' one of the Little Folk asked her
out of the side of her mouth. ' For you seem a fine lady
in your rich velvet gown and beautiful jewels, and should
have nothing to weep for.'

' Alas, good folk, my husband has gone away on a
journey, and when he comes back I must have spun for
him a hundred hanks of fine thread—or, dear as I am to
his heart, he will surely kill me and find another wife.
And I weep because I am not able to spin one good hank
of thread, let alone a hundred; and so I cannot do his
bidding.'

Then the six wee ladies looked at one another out of
their sharp bright eyes, and they all burst into lop-sided
laughter.

' Och, is that all your trouble ? ' said Whippety
Stourie. ' You can forget your sorrow, fair lady, for
we will help you. If you ask us to take supper with you
in your fine house on the day appointed for your husband's return, you will find that you will have nothing
more to worry about.'

The lady looked at the six wee folk in their gowns of
green, and she felt an upspringing of hope.

' Indeed, you are welcome to take supper in our house
on the day that my husband returns,' she said. ' And if
only you can help me, I will be grateful to you as long as I
live.'

Then she took her leave of them and rolled back the
flat grey stone so that it once more concealed the entrance
to their green cave in the hill-side. When she returned
to her house, she sat no more at her spinning-wheel, and
left untouched the heap of shining flax that lay in her

room—for she knew that the Little Folk would keep their word and come to help her.

Her husband came riding home in the evening of the day appointed for his return. He greeted his wife fondly and seemed to have left his glouchy humour behind him on his travels. At every moment his lady was expecting him to ask her about her spinning; but he did not have time to do so before the servants announced that supper was ready.

'Why are there six more places made ready at the table, and six wee stools drawn up beside them?' her husband asked as they sat down.

'Och, I asked six wee ladies to come and take supper with us tonight, for I thought the company would cheer you on your return,' the lady replied.

She had no sooner spoken than there was a scuttering of feet in the passage outside, and in came the six wee ladies in their gowns of green. The husband greeted them courteously, and bade them be seated. During the meal he talked and joked with them in high good humour, and his wife was pleased to see how well they agreed. Then there was a pause in their talk, and the husband looked at the six wee ladies curiously.

'Would you mind telling me,' he asked them, 'why it is that your mouths are all as lop-sided as a fir-tree leaning against the wind?'

Then the six wee ladies burst into loud, lop-sided laughter, and Whippety Stourie herself replied:

'Och, it's with our constant spin-spin-spinning. For we're all of us great ones for the spinning, and there's no surer way to a lop-sided mouth.'

At these words the husband grew pale. He looked at his fair wife, and he glanced at the wee ladies, and his alarm was plain to see.

And when their six wee guests had taken their leave

and departed, he put his arm round his lady's shoulders and called the servants to him.

'Burn the spinning-wheel that is in my wife's room,' he told them, 'and see that it perishes on a bright flame. I would not have my fair lady spin one more inch of thread, for fear she should spoil her bonny face. For there's no surer way to a lop-sided mouth than a constant spin-spin-spinning.'

The lady's heart leapt for joy at her husband's words; and from that day onwards the two of them lived contentedly for the rest of their days, with never the clack of a shuttle to disturb their happiness.

The White Pet

IN a grey stone farm-house that lay huddled in a valley below the heather-covered hills, there once lived a farmer who owned a fine sheep—or a White Pet, as they called a sheep in his part of Scotland. This White Pet was indeed a fine, plump beast, with a thick curling fleece; and when Christmas drew near, the farmer said to his wife:

' Tomorrow I will kill our White Pet, for it will give us a good Christmas dinner, and meat for many weeks to come. And you, dear wife, will be able to spin the thick curling fleece and weave it into fine woollen cloth.'

Now the White Pet overheard the farmer's words, and decided then and there that it was high time he left the farm-house in the valley and went out into the world to seek his fortune. So that very night, when the farmer and his wife were fast asleep, he ran away up the snow-covered hill-side as fast as his four legs could carry him.

He had not gone very far over the other side when a vast shape with two curving horns in front appeared out of the darkness, and he saw a red bull standing before him.

' Why are you out on the snow-covered hill-side on this cold winter's night, Bull ? ' asked the White Pet.

' Alas,' answered the Bull, ' my master was going to kill me for Christmas, and so I decided it was high time I came out into the world to seek my fortune.'

And he lifted up his head and bellowed loudly.

' Och,' said the White Pet, ' that is exactly what has happened to me. Let us go and seek our fortunes together.'

And so the two of them went on their way. They had not gone much farther when a sorry figure came shambling towards them with its tail between its legs, and they saw a big black dog standing before them.

' Why are you out on the snow-covered hill-side on this cold winter's night, Dog ? ' asked the White Pet.

' Alas,' answered the Dog, ' my master thought I was too old to work for him any longer, and was going to kill me, and so I decided it was high time I came out into the world to seek my fortune.'

And he barked, showing his sharp teeth.

' Och,' said the White Pet, ' that is exactly what has happened to us. Will you not join us so that we may all seek our fortunes together ? '

And so the three of them went on their way. After a little while a sinewy shape moved silently by, and they saw a cat standing before them.

' Why are you out on the snow-covered hill-side on this cold winter's night, Cat ? ' asked the White Pet.

' Alas,' answered the Cat, ' my mistress had no food to give me, and said she must drown me rather than let me starve. And so I decided it was high time I came out into the world to seek my fortune.'

And she miaowed, while her green eyes glinted.

' Och,' answered the White Pet, ' that is exactly what

has happened to us. Will you not join us so that we may all seek our fortunes together ? '

And so the four of them went on their way. Before long they met a plumed shape that strutted across their path, and they saw a cock standing before them.

' Why are you out on the snow-covered hill-side on this cold winter's night, Cock ? ' asked the White Pet.

' Alas,' answered the Cock, ' for a long time my master has been fattening me up to kill me for Christmas, and so I decided it was high time I came out into the world to seek my fortune.'

And he crowed, while his bright-red comb flopped over one beady eye.

' Och,' said the White Pet, ' that is exactly what has happened to us. Will you not join us so that we may all seek our fortunes together ? '

And so the five of them went on their way. They had only gone a short distance when a waddling figure came into their midst, and they saw a goose standing before them.

' Why are you out on the snow-covered hill-side on this cold winter's night, Goose ? ' asked the White Pet.

' Alas,' answered the Goose, ' my brother was killed at Easter, and my sister was killed at Michaelmas, and since it is nearly Christmas and I was left all alone in the pen, I decided it was high time I came out into the world to seek my fortune.'

And he opened his beak wide and gobbled.

' Och,' said the White Pet, ' that is exactly what has happened to us. Will you not join us so that we may all seek our fortunes together ? '

And so the six travellers—the White Pet, the Bull, the Dog, the Cat, the Cock, and the Goose—all set off in one company to seek their fortunes. The sky was still pitchy black, and they went carefully behind one another

so that they should not get lost.   Suddenly, overtopping
a little hill, they saw in the distance a square of light which
cast a guiding beam over the ground, making the snow
crystals glister and sparkle.   With one accord they
followed the beam, and soon found themselves before
the lighted window of a lonely house.

'Let us look inside the window,' said the White Pet,
'for doubtless it is here that we shall find our fortunes.'

Then the Cock spread his wings and perched himself
on the Bull's shoulder, so that he could tell his companions what was happening inside the house.

'What do I see,' he said excitedly, 'but six ugly
robbers standing round a table, counting out a great heap
of golden money !'

'Did I not say,' replied the White Pet, 'that it was
here we should find our fortunes ?'

Then he told his companions to raise a great shout,
each one uttering his own call at the same time, so that
the robbers would run away out of the house and leave
their gold behind them.   So all together, the White
Pet bleated, the Bull bellowed, the Dog barked, the Cat
miaowed, the Cock crowed, and the Goose gobbled—
and it was a mighty noise indeed that they raised, which
sounded like this :

'GAIRE !'

No sooner had their cry gone forth than the robbers
came rushing from the house, all six tumbling out on each
other's heels as though the devil himself was after them.
They ran into a nearby wood, and the animals entered
the house in triumph.   They found the golden money
left just as it was, all heaped upon the table, and when it
was divided out among them according to their satis-
faction, they settled themselves comfortably, blew out the
light, and prepared to sleep the rest of the night away.

The Bull stood behind the door; the White Pet stayed in the middle of the floor; the Dog lay down before the remains of the peat fire; the Cat curled up on the candle-

press; the Cock flew up to perch in the rafters; and the Goose settled himself in the midden just beyond the door.

Outside in the wood, the robbers saw the light go out, and when they heard no further sounds coming from the house, their leader decided to go back and see if he could retrieve the gold. He left his fellows among the trees, and stealthily entered through the door of the house. Nothing stirred in the darkness all about him, so he went over to where he knew the candle-press stood to get a light. But when he put forth his hand and took a candle, the Cat clawed him and he let out a great yell. Shaking with fright, he went over to the faintly glowing ashes of the fire to light the candle; but he had no sooner set a flame to the wick than the Dog got up, dipped his tail in a water-pot that stood by the hearth-side, and put

G

out the candle. Then the robber was truly terrified, and imagining that the house had been taken over by demons, he rushed towards the door. But on his way out, the White Pet hit him a mighty blow, the Bull gave him a kick, the Cock crowed loudly from the rafters, and the Goose set about him and beat him soundly with his wings as he stumbled, bruised and shaken, through the midden.

When he rejoined his comrades, they asked him how he had fared, and why he had come away without the gold.

' It's a wonder you see me before you at all,' he moaned. ' For I thought my last hour had come. I had no sooner got into the house, and reached up to take a candle, than a man in the candle-press thrust ten sharp knives into my hand. I had just managed to light the candle at the fire when a huge black rogue sprinkled water over it and drenched the flame. Then another ruffian rose up in the middle of the floor and gave me a mighty blow; a great villain behind the door kicked me right over the threshold, a shrill-voiced child of evil in the loft called out: ' *Cuir-anees-an-shav-ay-s-foui-mi-hayn-da !* ' (' Send him up here, and I'll do for him ! ')—and out in the midden a rascally shoemaker set about be-labouring me with his leather apron. And as for the gold—if you want it, you can get it yourselves; for I shall never enter that house again so long as I live.'

But his companions, hearing his tale, gave one glance of terror towards the house, and then all six of them turned and fled, and never rested the soles of their feet until they had put the distance of a great valley and two hill-sides between themselves and that fearful house.

As for the animals, they slept in peace until the day came; and since they found each other good company and had discovered as much fortune as anyone who sets out into the world can hope to come across, they decided to spend the rest of their lives together and stay where they were. And for all I know, they are living there still.

The Fox and the Little Bannock

THERE was once a good housewife who lived in a little white cottage at the top of a steep hill. One day she made three bannocks for her husband's supper: a big bannock, a middle-sized bannock, and a little bannock; and when she had taken them out of the oven, she put them on a platter to cool. The big bannock and the middle-sized bannock were quite content to remain where they were; but the little bannock, who was baked brown and crusty and smelt very good to eat, thought to himself:

'Why should I remain here and be eaten by the good man for his supper? I will go out into the world and seek a better fortune.'

So he jumped right off the platter and rolled to the cottage door. Now, as I have said, the cottage stood at the top of a steep hill; and before he could stop to think, the little bannock found himself rolling-rolling-rolling all the way down it.

'That was a quick escape, and no mistake!' he puffed. And then he gasped in dismay. For a river ran by the foot of the hill, and there was no way to get across it.

Just then who should come into sight but the red-brown fox, with his sharp white teeth and crafty eyes.

'Good day, little bannock,' said the Fox. 'Can it be that you are wanting to cross to the other side of the river?'

'Good day, Fox,' replied the little bannock a wee bit nervously, for the Fox had such *very* sharp white teeth, and his eyes were *so* crafty. 'Indeed, I am wanting to cross to the other side of the river.'

'I will take you over,' said the Fox.

'Och, no!' said the little bannock. 'If I were to let you do that, you would eat me for sure.'

'Eat you!' replied the Fox, pretending to be hurt at such a suggestion. 'Of course I won't eat you. Come on to the tip of my tail, and I will swim across the water.'

Well now, the little bannock thought that he surely ought to be safe enough if he was carried over like that; so he jumped on to the very tip of the Fox's bushy red brush, and they plunged into the river together.

When they were about a quarter of the way across, the water got deeper, and the Fox said:

'Come on to my back, little bannock, for you are getting wet.'

And the little bannock hopped on to the Fox's back.

When they were half-way across, the water grew deeper yet, and the Fox said:

'Come and perch between my ears, little bannock, for you are getting wet.'

And the little bannock hopped up between the Fox's ears.

When they were three-quarters of the way across, the water was the deepest it had ever been, and the Fox said:

'Come on to my nose, little bannock, for you are getting wet.'

And the little bannock hopped on to the tip of the Fox's long, pointed nose. Oh, foolish little bannock!

For the Fox immediately threw back his head and snapped him all up.   And by the time the farther side of the river was reached, there was only the crafty old Fox licking his lips with his long pink tongue, and no sign at all of the crusty little brown bannock who had tasted so very good to eat !

The Cock and the Fox

ONE day the red-brown Fox with his crafty eyes and bushy tail came slinking over the hill-side and stole away a fine, plump Cock from the farmer's yard.

At once there was a terrible commotion, and all the people came running out to chase the Fox, who set off for his lair as fast as he could go, with the Cock held firmly in his mouth.

Now Cockie-leerie-law was quite determined that he would not become the Fox's dinner, and he tried to think of a way to get the thief to open his mouth and let him fall. So he spoke up in a flattering tone and said:

' Are they not foolish, Fox, to be chasing the likes of you ! For they can never hope to catch up with you.'

The Fox was pleased at these words, for he was vain as well as crafty; and Cockie-leerie-law continued:

' All the same, although they cannot hope to catch you, it is not the thing at all to have a whole lot of people running along behind and crying " Stop, thief ! " Why do you not call out to them: " It is my own cock that is here, and not one that I have stolen at all ! " Then they will all turn back and you will be able to go on your way in peace.'

The Fox thought this was a very good idea, and without more ado he opened his mouth, threw up his head and sang out:

' Shê-mo-haolach-ha-n-a-han ! '

And while he did so, Cockie-leerie-law seized his opportunity and, with his bright-red comb flopping over one bright eye, ran straight back to the farm-yard.

The Fox and the Bird

A KESTREL hawk was dozing on the sun-warmed stones of a river-bank when the cunning red-brown Fox slunk upon him unawares, and with one pounce caught and held him in cruel jaws.

'Oh! Don't devour me,' cried the Hawk; 'if you will only let me go, I will lay for you an egg as big as your head!'

At this the Fox thought he had indeed got hold of a bird of birds; and, eager to have such a marvellous treasure for himself, he immediately loosened his grasp of the bird's soft throat.

Forthwith the kestrel flew up into the safety of a leafy tree-branch, where, safe from further injury, he began to mock the foolish Fox.

'I will not lay for you an egg as big as your head,' said the bird, 'for I cannot do it. But I will give you three pieces of advice, and if you will observe them, they will do you more good in the future.

'First: never believe an unlikely story from an unreliable authority. Second: never make a great fuss about a small matter. And third '—the bird looked down at the hungry Fox and paused—' third: whatever you get a hold of, take a firm grip of it.'

And saying this, he flew away and left the Fox with empty jaws.

Ainsel

THERE was once a small boy called Parcie who, like many other boys and girls, always made a great fuss when it was time for him to go to bed. He and his mother lived in a little stone cottage in the Border country; and although they were poor people with few worldly possessions, yet at night, when the fire was brightly burning in the hearth and their candle shone out with a kindly light, you could not have wished to be in a more comfortable or home-like place.

Parcie would sit by the fireside, maybe listening while his mother told him one of the old tales, or perhaps just drowsily watching the changing patterns in the glowing fire. By and by—but always too soon for Parcie's liking—his mother would say:

'It's time you were away to your bed, Parcie '—and after Parcie had protested a dozen times or more that it was too early yet, away he would go to his wee box-bed, to fall asleep as soon as he laid down his head.

One night, however, Parcie's mother got out of patience with listening to his protests, and as he obstinately refused to move from the fireside, she at last took up the candle and went off to bed herself, leaving him to his own devices.

'Very well; stay there if you will, Parcie,' she said as she went out the room. 'And if the auld faery-wife comes to take you away, it will be your own fault for disobeying me.'

'Faugh, what do I care for the auld faery-wife?' Parcie thought scornfully; and still he stayed where he was.

Now in common with many homesteads and farm-houses in those days, there was a brownie who used to come down the chimney of the cottage every night, to sweep the room and make everything spick and span. Parcie's mother always placed a bowl of goat's cream by the cottage door in return for the brownie's service, and in the morning it would be quite empty. These house-brownies were friendly creatures, though quick to take offence if they imagined themselves slighted in any way. Alas for the housewife who forgot to leave the brownie his bowl of cream! For the next morning she would find a room turned topsy-turvy, and the brownie would never return to help her again.

But the brownie who came to help Parcie's mother always found his bowl of cream waiting for him; and so he never failed to do his work neatly and silently while Parcie and his mother were fast asleep. He had, how-ever, a cross-tempered old faery mother, who was always at odds with the mortal race; and it was this auld faery-wife that Parcie's mother had spoken of when she went off to bed.

For a while Parcie remained contentedly by the hearth-side, happy to have won his own way; but when the fire began to lose its brightness, he shivered a little and thought longingly of his warm bed. He was just about to get up from the fireside when there was a sudden

scuffling and scraping in the chimney, and down into
the room jumped the brownie. Parcie was as surprised
to see him appear so unexpectedly as the brownie was
astonished to find Parcie not yet in his bed. After
staring at the spindle-legged, pointy-eared creature for a
few moments, Parcie said:

' What is your name ? '

' Ainsel (own self),' replied the brownie with a mis-
chievous grin. ' What's yours ? '

Parcie knew the brownie was joking, and he decided
to be cleverer still.

' *My* Ainsel,' he answered.

Then Parcie and the brownie played together by the
fireside. Ainsel was a lively creature, and Parcie
watched in amazement as he jumped from the high
wooden dresser on to the table, agile as a cat, and tumbled
his creels all over the floor. After a while Parcie stirred
up the remains of the fire, and to his dismay a glowing
cinder fell out on to the brownie's foot. At once
Ainsel set up such a yelling and screeching that the auld
faery-wife heard him and called down the chimney.

' Tell me who has hurt you,' she shouted fiercely,
' and I'll come down and do for him.'

At this Parcie ran out of the door and crept into his
wee box-bed in the adjoining room, pulling the blanket
over his head and quaking with fright.

" It was My Ainsel ! ' shrieked the brownie.

' Then what's all the fussing about ? ' the auld faery-
wife demanded, ' and how dare you disturb me with your
noise all over nothing ? There's no one to blame but
thine ainsel ! '

And a long, scrawny arm with claw-like fingers
reached down the chimney and snatched up the brownie
from the hearth-side.

In the morning, Parcie's mother found the bowl of

goat's cream she had set by the door untouched; and much to her bewilderment, the brownie never came to the cottage again.   But although she had lost her wee faery helper, she was delighted to find that after that night Parcie never had to be told twice to go to bed. For who knows?   The next time that long, scrawny arm with the claw-like fingers reached down the chimney it might be to snatch his own self up and away !

The Faery and the Kettle

SANDRAY is a little island in the Outer Hebrides, set
south of Barra and surrounded by the wide Atlantic
Ocean. The white-topped waves swirl round it,
and there's always a snell salt wind that blows about its
shore. Over it fly the shrill sea-birds: the plaintive
seagull, and the oyster-catcher who flies with his breast
and wings outstretched in a white cross, and cries: ' Bi
glic, bi glic, bi glic ! (' Be wise; be prudent; take care.')

Here there lived once a herd's wife called Mairearad,
who made friends with a Woman of Peace, which is one
of the names of the Faery Folk. (And sometimes they
are called Good Neighbours, and sometimes the Little
People.)

This faery was a wee slip of a woman, with a pointed
face and bright eyes and skin as brown as a hazel nut,
and she lived in a green grassy knoll that rose near by the
herd's cottage. Every day she would be coming along
the path that led to Mairearad's cottage door, and she
would walk straight inside and take away the big black
kettle from off the peat-turf fire. Never a word she

99

spoke, but as she left the cottage Mairearad would say to her:

> *'A smith is able to make*
> *Cold iron hot with a coal :*
> *The due of the kettle is bones,*
> *And to bring it back again whole.'*

And every night, the kettle would be left on the cottage doorstep, filled with juicy bones.

It happened one day that Mairearad had to cross the water to Castlebay, which is the big town on Barra; and early in the morning she said to her husband before she left:

' When the Woman of Peace comes, tell her that I am away at Castlebay, and let her take away the kettle as she always does.'

Then she set out, leaving her good man alone in the cottage. It was not long before the sound of light footsteps came to his ears, and he looked up from the heather-rope he was spinning to see the Woman of Peace approaching. And suddenly a strange fear fell upon him; his mind filled with all the tales he had ever heard of the spells and enchantments that the Faery Folk can cast upon a mortal—and, leaping to his feet, he slammed shut the cottage door just as the Woman of Peace reached the threshold.

Now anger comes swiftly to the Little People, for they are quick to take offence; and at once the faery's bright eyes grew brighter yet with anger at the herd's churlishness. She set her foot on the window-ledge and climbed up to the chimney hole in the middle of the roof, and there she gave one weird, shrill screech.

And the herd, huddling against the door in terror, saw the great black kettle give two jumps upon the fire, and fly straight up the chimney, where it disappeared in the grasp of a skinny brown hand. It was a long time

before he dared open the cottage door again; and when
he did so, there was no sign at all of the faery.

In the evening, when Mairearad returned from
Castlebay with the basket over her arm full of fresh
herring, the first thing she did was to ask her husband
why the kettle was not back in its place on the fire.

' For the Woman of Peace has always returned it before
darkness falls,' she said. ' It is not like herself to be
forgetting it.'

Then her husband told her what had happened while
she was away; and when the tale was done, Mairearad
scolded him with a sharp tongue for his foolishness.
And at once she rose up and took the lantern in her hand,
and hastened to the green knoll where the faery lived.
There, at the foot of the moonlit slope, she found her
kettle, filled as usual with juicy bones. She stooped and
picked it up, and set off home again: but as soon as she
turned her face towards her cottage, a faery voice cried
out:

> ' *Silent wife, silent wife,*
> *That came on us from the land of chase,*
> *Thou man on the surface of the Brugh,*
> *Loose the Black and slip the Fierce.*'

Forthwith a wild shriek echoed from the top of the
knoll, and a dark figure standing there let slip two faery
hounds that crouched by his side. They came bounding
down the hill-side, baying loud and long; and their tails
were curled over their green backs, and their tongues
hung over their pointed teeth.

When Mairearad heard the sound of their pursuit, she
gave one terrified glance across her shoulder and broke
into a panic-stricken flight. For the faery hounds will
overtake and devour any living creature within their path.
And fast as she fled, faster yet the two green dogs came
after her, till the breath of them tickled her heels and she

H

thought to feel their teeth close round her ankle-bones at the very next moment. Then she remembered the juicy bones that lay in her kettle, and a sudden idea came to her. In desperation she put her hand inside the kettle and flung all the bones behind her as she ran.

Immediately the faery hounds seized on them greedily; and breathing thanks for this small delay in their pursuit, Mairearad at last came within sight of her cottage. Yet as she drew near the door, she heard them coming after her again; and she used her last breath in a desperate cry for her good man to let her in. Even as she fell across the threshold and he shut fast the door, there was a fierce noise of scrabbling on the wood, and a furious howl rent the air.

All through the night Mairearad and her husband sat up in terror; and when the next day dawned bright and peaceful, and they at last found courage to look outside the cottage door, they saw how deeply it had been scored by the faery hounds, and how fiercely it had been scorched by their fiery breath.

Never again did the Woman of Peace come to borrow Mairearad's kettle; and although they have now lain beneath God's acre for many a year, for so long as they lived, the herd and his wife were careful to avoid all further contact with the Faery Folk.

Morag and the Water Horse

WHEN the warm days come and the sun begins to burn the bracken brown, according to their age-old custom the Highland crofters take their cattle to summer pastures in the hills, re-opening the shielings where they will stay until it is time to return home again.

Many years ago there lived a crofter called Donald MacGregor, whose summer shieling lay on a lonely slope of hill-side overlooking a great loch. His little white cabin stood as a haven in the midst of the heather, and the lush grass that grew on the lower land provided rich pasture for his cattle. And yet there were many people who shook their heads and called Donald Mac-Gregor a foolish man to have built his shieling in that place; and there was no one who would set out along the path that led there once dusk had fallen upon the earth. This was because a dreaded monster lived in the depths of the great loch near by, preying upon the hill-side round about: a Water Horse.

No man could describe the appearance of the monster. Those who had stayed long enough to catch more than a glimpse of the terrible creature as it rose from the dark waters of the loch had not lived to tell the tale; while as it roamed the hill-side, it was able to assume any form at will (for it was full of evil enchantment) and might appear as an aged woman, a black raven, or perhaps a cunning-eyed fox, only resuming its own shape when it was near enough to seize and mercilessly devour its prey. But it was said that the Water Horse was huge and black; that two sharp, satanic horns sprang from its monstrous head; and that it could outstrip the wind as it plunged through the heather.

But in spite of the tales that were told of this fearsome creature, and although each year the Water Horse claimed another victim for its own, Donald MacGregor took no notice when his neighbours warned him of the danger of having his shieling so near the loch, advising him to move across the burn that trickled by its side—for it was known that a Water Horse might never cross over running water, and all land beyond the burn was safe. Donald only replied that his cattle should have the richest pasture he could find for them, which happened to be on the very borders of the loch, and that he would believe in the existence of the Water Horse when he met it face to face. As for the monster's luckless victims, he swore that their disappearance was really due to the fact that they had availed themselves too freely of their neighbours' hospitality, and in the dark had stumbled and fallen over a precipice along their homeward path.

Yet in the end he was forced to take back his scornful words; and this is the way it happened.

He had one daughter called Morag, whom he loved dearly. Each year she used to accompany her father to their summer dwelling, and all through the long, light days she would sit at the door of the shieling with her spinning-wheel. Then, as approaching darkness deepened the purple shadows in the heather, she would go down to the lochside to call in the cattle. As she went barefooted over the hill, she told herself that there was nothing to fear; for had not her father told her that she should not be afraid? And yet she shivered as the waters of the loch lapped against their grassy margins, and peered distrustfully into the shadows cast by the rowan-trees that grew there. But always she returned safely, and in the daytime frightened fancies fled away, and Morag would sing as she sat spinning in the sun.

One golden morning as she was turning her shuttle without a care in the world, a dark shadow came between herself and the sunlight, and she broke off her song with a scream.

' I did not mean to startle you,' said a pleasant voice; and looking round, Morag discovered a young man standing beside her. He was tall and comely, and there was the look of strength on his broad shoulders. Yet his appearance was strange, for his clothes and hair were dark and dripping with water.

' How is it you are so wet ? ' asked Morag. ' For there is not a cloud to be seen in the sky.'

' For sure,' the young man answered easily, ' the sole of my foot slipped as I passed by a tarn high in the hills, and I fell into the water. The sun will soon dry me.'

He sat on the ground by Morag's side, and she was not loth to let her spinning-wheel hang idle while he spoke fair words to her. Yet in spite of the charm in his manner, his pleasant speech, and tender glances, Morag could not help feeling that there was something strange about him, although she tried to push this thought away from her mind.

As he felt the sunlight on his scalp, the young man brushed one hand over his damp head.

' Lay your head upon my lap,' said Morag, ' and let me smooth your hair.'

And while the young man did as she bade him, she began to comb his dark locks with gentle hands.   But suddenly she paused in her combing, and terror entered her soul.

For she saw that the teeth of the comb were choked with fine green strands of weed and grains of silt.   That weed and silt she knew well, for had she not seen it often in her father's net when he fished in the great loch below the hill-side?   In truth, it was the *liobhagach an locha* that was wrapped round the roots of the young man's hair. . . . Young man?   This was no young man, but the dreaded Water Horse itself, risen from its lair and present in this comely shape to lure her to her death.

At this moment the monster saw the great fear in Morag's eyes.   With a terrible scream she pushed the dark head away from her and sprang to her feet.   The spinning-wheel toppled to the ground as she fled away and away down that steep hill-side, with the wings of terror on the heels of her.   And behind, dreadful in the sunlight, spread a great shadow that was darker than the deepest waters of the great loch itself.

But Morag was more fortunate than many another who had been marked out as a victim by the Water Horse, for the monster did not succeed in overtaking her before she reached the little burn that trickled by the side of the loch; and once she had leaped across its running water, she was safely out of danger.

Never again did any man enter the door of the white shieling above that haunted loch—not even Donald MacGregor, who was so shaken by his daughter's peril that he took back every word he had ever spoken in derision of the Water Horse.   And to this day you may see the scattered stones of the ruined cabin lying in the midst of the curling bracken.

The Smith and the Faeries

AT Caonisgall on the Isle of Islay there once lived a smith called Alasdair MacEachern, who was known as Alasdair of the Strong Arm. He lived in a stone cottage next door to his forge, alone with his son Neil; for his wife had died when the child was born, leaving the two of them to comfort each other. Neil was a slightly built youth with a depth of dreaming in his eyes and a gentle manner; but for all that, he promised well as his father's apprentice in the forge. Alasdair's neighbours warned him to take good care of his son until he should reach man's estate; for Neil was just such a mortal as the Little Folk loved to steal away to their Land of Light, to become one of their own fair company and dance his life away.

Alasdair took good notice of his neighbours' counsel, and every evening he hung a branch of rowan above the doorway of the cottage; for this was a sure charm against the power of the Little Folk.

One day he had to go on a journey which meant spending the night away from his home; and before he left he said to his son:

' Be sure you remember to place a rowan branch above the cottage door this night; for then there will be no chance of the Little Folk taking you away to join their company.'

Neil nodded, and said he would remember this, and Alasdair of the Strong Arm went off on his journey.

After he had swept the cottage and milked the goat and given some corn to the fowls, Neil wrapped six oat-cakes and a slice of goat's cheese in a cloth and spent the day on the fells, where he loved to feel the springy heather underfoot and listen to the little streams channelling their way down the hill-side. He wandered far, eating his oat-cakes and cheese when he felt hungry; and by the time he came home again, night had fallen and he was weary. He flung himself down to sleep in his box-bed in the corner without a thought for the branch of rowan that he should have hung above the door; for he had completely forgotten his father's parting words.

When Alasdair returned to his cottage the next day, he found the fire unlaid and the floor unswept, with the door standing open over the threshold. The goat had not been milked, and the cock and the hens had been given no corn; and when he called to his son to see why this state of affairs had come about, a thin, unnatural voice answered him from the box-bed in the corner.

' Here I am, father, still in my bed. An illness has fallen upon me, and I must stay here until I am well again.'

Alasdair was very alarmed by these words, and when he approached the bed he was shocked to see how much his son had changed in such a short time. He lay thin and wasted under the blanket; his skin had become yellow and wrinkled; and there was a strange look of age about him, for all that he was but a youth. He remained in this condition for several days, showing no improvement, in spite of the fact that he seemed suddenly to have developed an enormous and insatiable appetite, and would be eating all the day long. Alasdair was at his wits' end to know what to do when an old man who had a great reputation for knowledge and wisdom (which are two very different things) walked into the cottage. He hailed the old man gladly, for he hoped that he would be able to tell him what was the matter with his son ; and while he described the trouble that had fallen upon the boy, the old man listened gravely, nodding his head now and then. When Alasdair had finished talking and the two of them had looked at the boy, they walked a little way outside the cottage, and then the old man said :

'You are asking me what it is that ails your son— but I am telling you that it is not your son that is there at all. He has been carried off by the *Daoine Sith* (Little People) while you were away from home, and they have left a *sibhreach* (changeling) in his place.'

Alasdair looked at the old man in dismay.

'Alas, what then shall I do ? ' he said. 'And shall I ever see my son again ? '

'I will tell you what it is you must do,' the old man replied. 'But first, to make sure that it is indeed a *sibhreach* that is lying in your son's bed, you must go back into the cottage and gather together as many empty egg-shells as you can find. Spread them out carefully in the changeling's sight, then fill them with water, and, carrying them as if they were a heavy weight, arrange them with a great show of deliberation about the fire-side.'

Alasdair listened carefully to this strange counsel, then went into the cottage to carry out the old man's instructions. He had not been long at the work when a sudden screech of laughter came from the box-bed in the corner, and the high-pitched voice of the creature he had mistaken for his son cried out:

' I am now eight hundred years of age, and I have never seen the like of that before ! '

Alasdair returned to the old man and told him of this, and the old man said:

' It is without doubt a *sibhreach* that has changed places with your son. You must get rid of him as soon as possible, and then I think I can help you to find your son again. You must now light a very large, bright fire before the bed on which this creature is lying. He will ask you, " What is the use of that ? " Answer him at once—" You will see presently." Then seize him and throw him into the middle of the flames—and he will fly out through the cottage roof.'

Once again Alasdair returned to the cottage and carried out the old man's instructions. He kindled a fire before the changeling's bed, and sure enough the high-pitched voice asked:

' What is the use of that ? '

' You will see presently,' replied the smith—and then he suddenly seized the creature and flung him on top of the flames. The *sibhreach* gave a terrible yell, and springing up on his thin yellow shanks, he flew right through the roof, where there was a hole to let out the smoke, and disappeared entirely.

' And now what should I do ? ' Alasdair asked the old man. ' For I would be seeking my son without delay.'

' It is into the round green hill that lies yonder they have taken your son,' the old man told him, pointing to the grassy knoll behind the smith's cottage. ' For that is a faery dwelling-place. On the night of the next full moon the door of the hill-side will be open, and it is then that you must go to seek your son. Take up your

Bible, your dirk, and your crowing cock, and enter the hill.   You will hear singing and merriment, and you will see dancing and a great blaze of light.   But when you have stuck your dirk in the threshold of the hill to prevent the door from closing upon you—for the faeries may not touch cold steel that has been forged by mortal hands—advance boldly and without fear.   Your Bible will protect you from all dangers.

' You will soon find yourself in a wide room, and at one end you will see your son working at a forge.   When you are questioned by the Little Folk, you must say you have come to seek him, and will not go away without him.'

And forthwith the old man took his leave, followed along his way by the gratitude and goodwill of the smith.

Now Alasdair was not only strong of arm, but strong of courage too; and he waited impatiently until it should be time for him to go forth and seek his son according to the old man's counsel.   When the moon had waned, and waxed again, and once more stood full in the sky, he rose up from his cottage and made his way towards the green knoll on the hill-side.   His dirk was sheathed to his side; his Bible was clasped to his breast; and under his left arm he carried the cock, who was fast asleep.   As he drew nearer to the hill-side, it seemed to Alasdair that he could hear a faint sound of singing and revelry; and even as he waited by the very foot of the knoll itself, the sound became louder and the hill-side suddenly opened wide on a great blaze of light.   At once he sprang up and unsheathed his dirk, which he sent quivering into the threshold of the faery land, as he had been bidden.   Then he strode boldly into the blaze of light, still clasping his Bible to his breast and still carrying the sleeping cock under his left arm.   And when he had shouldered his way through the dance that has no end for mortal men until they find themselves on a sudden alone and old on the cold hill-side, Alasdair saw his son, pale and wild-eyed, working at a faery forge in the midst of a green-clad crowd of the Little Folk.

As soon as the faeries saw an intruder among their company, they clustered round to find out what mortal man had dared to trespass into their domain.   But none of them could come near Alasdair to harm him or charm him, because of the power of the Bible that he carried on his breast.   Then the smith faced his son, and cried out :

'Release my son from the enchantment you have cast over him, and let him return with me to his own people and his own land.'

Neil started at the sound of his father's voice.   The wildness left his eyes, and he took a step towards Alasdair, holding forth his arms in eagerness.   But the faery company burst into weird laughter at the smith's words, as if to mock at him for his hope of recovering his son.

Just at that moment—so quickly does time go by in the faery land according to a mortal's reckoning—the first light of dawn streaked over the hill-side, and the cock under Alasdair's arm stirred and awoke from sleep.   He stretched his neck, the brave red comb stood up from his head, and he gave one mighty crow to herald the coming of the new day.   At that fearsome sound, which is the faeries' curfew—for they may never be abroad in daylight —the mocking of the Little People was changed to consternation.   They pushed and pulled both Alasdair and his son towards the opening in the green hill-side, so that the smith might retrieve his dirk and the threshold of their land once more be hidden from the eyes of men. But even as Alasdair plucked up his dirk and the hill-side closed behind him and his son, one eldritch voice cried out:

' May your son never speak until the day he breaks the spell I set upon him now !   This is the faery curse that shall come upon him.'

A moment later, both the smith and his son found themselves back on their familiar hill-side in the clear light of early morning, with never a sign in the close-cropped grass around them to show where the entrance to that Land of Light had been.   They returned to their cottage, and Alasdair blew up the bellows in his forge again, while Neil helped him with his work as before. But a great sorrow was upon the smith, for from the time that Neil was delivered from the Little Folk, his lips remained sealed and he could not utter one word.   Thus was the faery curse fulfilled; and because he did not know by what means he might break the spell that was upon him, Neil looked to live in silence for the rest of his life.

A year and a day had gone by since his son's return, when Alasdair set to work to forge a new claymore for the Chief of his clan.   Neil helped his father in this task, holding the red-hot steel to the fire so that the blade would be keen and finely tempered; and all the while he said no word.

But just as his father had fairly set about fashioning the sword, a sudden memory of his brief stay in the faery land flashed into Neil's mind. He remembered the forge of the Little People, where glittering sparks flew all around, and he remembered how the faery smiths fashioned their bright swords, tempering the blades with charms as well as skill, to make an enchanted weapon that would never fail its owner. And while Alasdair stood aside in amazement, Neil took over the making of the Chief's claymore. Under his hands a weapon took shape that might well have come from the faery forge itself; and when it was finished, he stepped back and looked at his father in triumph.

' There is a sword that will never fail the man who grasps it by the hilt,' he said; and he spoke for the first time in a year and a day. For by good fortune, he had performed the very deed that could remove the curse of silence that lay upon him: the fashioning of a faery sword to sever a faery spell.

From that hour, all memory of the Land of Light went from the lad; and in time he succeeded his father as the finest smith in all his clan. As for the faery sword he had fashioned, the *Claidheamh Ceann-Ileach*, it was prized above all his Chief's possessions, for it never failed its owner in battle, and brought great victories and honour to the clan.

The Good Housewife and her Night Helpers

IN days gone by, thrifty housewives used to spin their wool and weave their cloth late at night, when they had finished their daytime work. This was the custom of Inary, the wife of a prosperous farmer who lived on Tiree, hard by a fair green mound called Burg Hill, which was known as a faery dwelling-place.

On a certain night as she sat spinning by candlelight after her husband and the rest of the household had gone off to bed, a great tiredness came upon Inary, and putting her hand to her brow she exclaimed aloud:

' Oh that someone would come from land or sea, from far or near, to help me with the work of making this cloth ! '

She had no sooner spoken, than she heard a knocking on the door, and a chanting voice called to her:

' Inary, good housewife, open the door to me; for I am come to help you in your work.'

Wonderingly Inary arose and opened the door; and there on the threshold was a strange wee slip of a woman dressed all in green. She entered the room and went straight to the spinning-wheel, where she began to ply the shuttle without further ado. Inary had no sooner shut the door behind her when there came a louder knocking, and another sing-song voice called out:

'Inary, good housewife, open your door; for I am come to help you in your work.'

And when Inary unlatched the door for the second time, another weird green woman came into the room, and took her place at the distaff.

But this was by no means the end of it, for hard on the heels of the second stranger came a third green woman, and then a fourth, a fifth, a sixth, and a seventh: until at last poor Inary lost all count of her visitors, and stood in helpless amazement, watching as they settled down with extraordinary eagerness to carding and teazing her wool; plying her weaving-shuttle quick and fast; thrumming her loom with restless fingers, and busily boiling the fulling water that was used to clean and thicken her homespun cloth.

'Surely it is all the faeries of Burg Hill who have come to my house this night!' she said to herself.

There was now such a din and clatter in the place, with the green-clad, dark-skinned little women jostling one another for elbow room, that it was a great wonder the good man who slept in the adjoining room was not awakened. Yet in spite of all, he slumbered with uncanny soundness through the uproar, and Inary began to fear that the little people had put spells on him. Meanwhile, her shrill-voiced helpers continually cried that they were hungry, and she endeavoured to get enough food prepared for them. And if she was tired before they came to do her work, she was now seven times as tired with trying to keep their mouths filled. As the night advanced, their enormous appetite seemed to keep pace with the fantastic speed of their labours; and it appeared that the universe itself could not keep them in meat and bread. By midnight, Inary was ready to drop down from her toiling, and her one thought was how she might rid herself of her faery visitors. It was in vain that she went into the adjoining room to try to wake her husband; she might as well have striven to rouse a millstone, for no matter how loudly she shouted in his ear, he did not stir.

When she was almost at her wits' end, she thought of going for advice to a certain wise man who lived near by. Leaving the green-clad ones eating her last baking of bread, with only a little bannock left toasting on the hearth, she slipped away and took the path to the old man's cottage, where she poured out all her trouble to him and implored his help.

' How can I get rid of the wee folk ? ' she asked him, ' and how can I waken my good man, who sleeps as though he is under spells ? '

The wise man chid her for her thoughtlessness in ever having asked for uncanny help from land or sea, from far or near, in the first place, and said:

' So long as you live, do not again wish, ask, or pray for that which you may regret having brought upon yourself. You are right in supposing your husband to be under spells; and before he can be awakened, your faery visitors must be got out of the house, and part of the fulling-water sprinkled over him. And the way you shall get rid of the wee folk is this:

' You must return to your house and, standing by the open door, cry out three times, as loud as you can: " Burg Hill is on fire ! " The green company will then leave their work and rush out to see if this is so. As soon as they are outside, you must shut the door and then set to and disarrange, reverse, overturn, and upset all the implements with which they have been working. The rest will look after itself.'

I

Thanking the old man for his good advice, Inary hastened back to her house. Reaching the open door, she cried out with all the strength she could muster:

' There is fire in Burg Hill! Burg Hill is on fire! Burg Hill is in red flames of fire ! '

Before she had finished uttering the third warning, out from the house rushed all the faery folk with one accord, crushing and trampling one another in their anxiety to be away. And as they went, each one of them cried for the things she held most dear, which lay in the faery hill:

> *' My husband and little ones,*
> *My cheese and butter-keg,*
> *My sons and daughters,*
> *My big meal chests,*
> *My comb and wool-cards,*
> *Thread and distaff,*
> *Cow and fetter,*
> *Horses and traces,*
> *Harrows and hoard,*
> *And the ground bursting,*
> *My hammers and anvil,*
> *Burg Hill is on fire,*
> *And if Burg Hill is burnt,*
> *My pleasant occupations*
> *And merriments are gone.'*

As soon as Inary saw that they were all out of the house, she went in quickly and shut the door. Then, as she had been told to do, she deranged everything with which the faeries had been working. She took the band off the spinning-wheel, twisted the distaff the opposite way, turned the loom topsy-turvy, and took the fulling-water off the fire. She had barely finished doing this when the faery company, having found out how she had tricked them into leaving the house, returned and knocked at the door, the blows of their knuckles coming as thick and fast as hail-stones in winter.

' Inary, good housewife, let us in ! ' they cried.

' I will not,' she replied.

So they called to the spinning-wheel to let them in.

' Good Spinning-wheel, get up and open the door for us.'

' How can I,' said the Spinning-wheel, ' when I am without a band ? '

They now appealed to the distaff.

' Good Distaff, open the door for us.'

' I would willingly do so,' replied the Distaff, ' but I am twisted contrary.'

Then they thought of the weaving-loom.

' Good Weaving-loom, open the door for us.'

' That I would do with pleasure, but I am turned topsy-turvy,' it answered them.

There was yet the fulling-water to call upon.

' Good Fulling-water, will you not open the door ? '

' I cannot, when I am off the fire,' said the Fulling-water.

The little folk were getting exhausted and impatient, and as a last resource they turned and besought the little bannock that was toasting on the hearth.

' Little Bannock of good fortune, open the door quickly ! '

The Little Bannock jumped up and hopped to the door as fast as it could; but the good housewife was quicker yet.　She ran after it and nipped it with her hands, so that it fell with a plop on the floor.

When they realized that there was indeed no way for them to enter the house, the faeries began shrieking and crying until their hubbub became unbearable.　Then at last Inary remembered what she had to do with the fulling-water, and taking a panful into the next room, she threw it over the good man, who awoke immediately. And high time it was too.　As soon as he heard the terrible noise going on outside, he rose up from his bed, flung open the door of the house, and stood on the threshold with a black frown on his face.

And immediately the uproar ceased and the wee folk faded away like green shadows, never to trouble Inary again.

The Adventures of Iain Direach

WHEN the world was much younger than it is nowadays, there lived a king's son who was known as Iain Direach, which means 'Upright John'. He was by way of being a great hunter, and one day when he was out over the hill-side with his bow and arrow, what should come flying overhead but the most beautiful bird he had ever seen in his life: a blue falcon. As quick as thought he loosed an arrow in the air; but the falcon outsped his shot, and only one blue feather came drifting to the ground. Iain picked up the feather, and when he reached home he showed it to his stepmother the Queen.

Now she was one who had the habit of bad magic, and as soon as she saw the feather she knew that it had fallen from the plumage of no ordinary bird at all. She was immediately filled with a great determination to have the blue falcon for her own; and she decided that her stepson, whom she hated in her heart, should get it for her, no matter what hardship or danger should befall him in the task. So she told Iain Direach to go forth and find the bird for her, and not to return without it; and because he feared the Queen's bad magic, Iain went out to do her bidding.

He journeyed back to the hill-side where he had seen the falcon; but although he strained his eyes to the farthest horizon, there was never a sign of the marvellous bird. Soon dusk descended on the earth, and the little fluttering birds of the hedgerow flew from the bush tops, from tuft to tuft, and to the briar roots, seeking their rest. And when the night came blind and dark, Iain settled down under a tree and kindled a fire to warm himself. He was just preparing to sleep as best he might when there was a rustling close beside him, and into the firelight stepped *An Gille Mairtean*, the red-brown Fox, carrying in his mouth a wether's trotter and a sheep's cheek.

' This is a poor night to be spending out of doors, king's son,' he greeted Iain.

' It is indeed,' Iain replied; ' but I am seeking the blue falcon for my stepmother the Queen, and I may not return to my home until I have found it.'

Then the Fox looked at Iain with the cunning wisdom of his kind and said:

' Your task is hard, but if you are careful it should not prove impossible.'

And while they shared the wether's trotter and the sheep's cheek for their supper—and Iain with a hunger inside him like a famished water-bull's—the Fox told him that the blue falcon belonged to the great Giant of the Five Heads, the Five Humps, and the Five Throttles.

' You must go to the Giant,' said the Fox, ' and seek service in his house, telling him that you are especially skilful in looking after all manner of birds. He will then put under your care all his hawks and falcons; and among them will be the bird you are seeking. Then, on a day when the Giant is away from home, it should be an easy enough matter for you to run off with the blue falcon. But remember this: while you are escaping from the Giant's house, on no account should so much as the tip of one blue wing-feather touch anything that is there. For if this happens, then it will not go well with you.'

Iain thanked the Fox for his counsel, and then the two of them spent the rest of the night under the tree. At dawn the next morning the Fox set Iain on his way to the Giant of the Five Heads, the Five Humps, and the Five Throttles. And if it was far that the tree-covered line of the horizon lay in front of him, it was farther yet to the Giant's house.

But when the sun was going down on the world he came to it at last; and when he knocked at the great door, it was opened by the Giant himself, who was such a terrible great man that Iain was in two minds whether or not to run back all the way that he had come.

'What do you want of me, king's son?' roared the awful one.

'I would be seeking service in your house,' replied Iain. 'And if it's any use to you at all, I've a great skill in looking after all manner of birds.'

'Then it's a day of days for myself that you've come to me,' replied the Giant, setting wide the door and inviting Iain into his house. 'For I'm wanting someone to look after my hawks and my falcons.'

So Iain found service with the Giant of the Five Heads, the Five Humps, and the Five Throttles; and sure enough, among the birds entrusted to his care was the blue falcon that his stepmother desired to have for her own. When he saw how well Iain looked after his birds, the Giant was content to leave him alone with them while he himself went out hunting; and on one such day, Iain decided to make good his escape.

He waited until the Giant's earth-shaking tread had

died away over the hill-side, then carefully lifted the blue
falcon from its perch.   Remembering the Fox's warning,
he carried the bird to the threshold as carefully as if it
were made of brittle glass.   But alas !   As soon as he
opened the door and the falcon saw the bright daylight,
it spread wide its wings, and the tip of one blue wing-
feather touched the door-post, which immediately sent
forth a screech that could have been heard a hundred
miles away or more.

Iain had no time to think what he should do next
before there was a mighty heaving of the ground, and
the Giant came running home over the hill-side.

' You are trying to steal my blue falcon from me ! '
he roared with the terrible strength of all his five voices.
' You are fleeing with that which is not yours ! '

' Forgive me ! ' cried Iain, ' but it was my stepmother
the Queen who sent me out to seek the bird for her, and I
may not return home without it.'

Then the Giant looked at Iain with a cunning light in
his ten eyes.

' I will give you my blue falcon,' he said, ' if you can
get for me the White Sword of Light that belongs to the
Big Women of Dhiurradh.'

And when Iain had promised to fulfil this mission and
had set out with a light step, the Giant leant against the
door-post and laughed and laughed with a laughter that
was like the echoing of thunder; for he thought that
Iain Direach would never be able to accomplish the task
he had set him.

Many miles Iain journeyed across the countryside
without resting the sole of his foot; but he met no one
who would tell him how to find the Big Women of
Dhiurradh.   When darkness came he kindled a fire under
the protection of a great tree, and was just settling down
to sleep as best he might when, as it had happened

before, there was a rustling close beside him, and who should step into the firelight but his old friend the Fox.

'So you did not succeed in bringing away the blue falcon from the Giant's house,' he greeted Iain.

'Alas, I did not,' replied Iain, 'but the Giant has said that he will give me the falcon if I will fetch for him the White Sword of Light that belongs to the Big Women of Dhiurradh.'

Then the Fox looked at Iain with the cunning wisdom of his kind and said:

'Your task is hard, but if you are careful it should not be impossible.'

And while they shared their supper as before, the Fox told him that Dhiurradh was an island that lay in the middle of the sea, and that the Big Women were three sisters who dwelt on it.

'You must go to them,' said the Fox, 'and seek service in their house, saying that you are especially skilled in the art of brightening and polishing all manner of metals. They will then give you the care of all their weapons, and among them will be the sword you are seeking. Then, on a day when they are away from home, it should be an easy enough matter for you to run off with it. But remember my previous warning, and while you are escaping do not let so much as the point of the blade touch anything that is in the house. For if this happens, then it will not go well with you.'

In the mouth of morning the two of them went down to a place where the ocean washed against the land, and then the Fox said:

'I will grow into a boat and take you to the island of Dhiurradh.'

And in the twinkling of an eye he changed himself into a narrow red-brown boat, and Iain rowed over the water until he came under the cliffs of a craggy island in

the middle of the sea.   As soon as the boat grounded on
the shore the Fox turned himself into his own shape again.

'Good luck attend you, king's son,' he said as Iain
set off by himself to find the house of the Big Women.
'And on the day that you escape I will be waiting here to
take you back over the water.'

It was but a little distance to the house, and when Iain
knocked on the great door it was opened by the three
sisters themselves.   The first was as tall as a fir-tree, the
second was as dark as a stormy day, and the third was as
ugly as a bad deed.

'What do you want of us, king's son?' they croaked.

'I would be seeking service in your house,' replied
Iain.   'And if it's any use to you at all, I've a great skill
in brightening and polishing all manner of metals.'

'Then it's a day of days for ourselves that you've come
to us,' replied the Big Women, setting wide the door
and inviting Iain into their house.   'For we're needing
someone to look after our swords and claymores.'

So Iain found service with the Big Women of
Dhiurradh; and sure enough, among the weapons
entrusted to his care was the White Sword of Light that
the Giant of the Five Heads, the Five Humps, and the
Five Throttles desired to have for his own.   When the
three sisters saw how well Iain looked after their weapons,
they were content to leave him alone in the house while
they themselves went abroad; and it was on such a day
that Iain decided to make good his escape.

As soon as the tall one, the dark one, and the ugly
one had made off for the other side of the island, he
carefully lifted the White Sword of Light from its place.
With the Fox's warning uppermost in his mind, he
carried it to the threshold.   But alas!   Just as he was
going through the door the very point of the blade
touched the lintel, which immediately sent forth a screech

that could have been heard a thousand miles away or more.

At once the three sisters came running home as fast as they could.

'You are trying to steal our White Sword of Light from us!' they screamed. 'You are fleeing with that which is not yours!'

'Forgive me!' cried Iain, 'but it was the Giant of the Five Heads, the Five Humps, and the Five Throttles who sent me out to seek it for him. For until I get it for him, he will not give me his blue falcon; and without the blue falcon I may not return home to my stepmother the Queen.'

Then the three Big Women looked at Iain with a crafty gleam in their eyes.

'We will give you our White Sword of Light,' they said, 'if you can get for us the Yellow Bay Filly that belongs to the King of Eirinn.'

And when Iain had promised to do their bidding and had set out with hope in his heart, the three Big Women fell upon each other's necks with hideous cackles of laughter; for they thought that Iain Direach would never be able to fulfil the task they had set him.

When he got down to the shore below the craggy cliffs, Iain found the Fox waiting there as he had promised.

'So you did not succeed in bringing away the White Sword of Light from the house of the Big Women of Dhiurradh,' he greeted him.

'Alas, I did not,' replied Iain; and he told the Fox that the sword would not be his until he had fetched to Dhiurradh the Yellow Bay Filly that belonged to the King of Eirinn.

Then the Fox looked at Iain with the cunning wisdom of his kind and said:

'Your task is hard, but if you are careful it should not

be impossible. Eirinn is a country that lies a little farther over the ocean, and I will grow into a bark and take you there. When we reach Eirinn, you must make your way to the royal palace and seek service there as the King's stable lad. Among the horses placed in your care will be the one you are seeking. And during the night, when everyone is asleep, it should be an easy enough matter for you to run off with the Yellow Bay Filly. But once again, make sure that while you are escaping, no part of the horse but the soles of its feet touch the inner side of the stable gate. For if this happens, it will not go well with you, as you have already learnt to your sorrow.'

Then without more ado the Fox turned into a bark with red-brown sails, and carried Iain over the water to the shores of the green land of Eirinn (Ireland). When they reached the end of their journey, the Fox turned himself into his own shape again and said:

' Good luck attend you, king's son. And on the night that you escape I will be waiting here to take you back across the water.'

Iain walked through the green countryside, and soon came to the royal palace; and when he knocked on the great door it was opened by the King of Eirinn himself.

' What do you want of me, stranger ? ' asked the King, who was a grand man dressed in rich garments.

' I would be seeking service as your stable lad,' replied Iain.

' Then it's a day of days that you've come here,' said the King, ' for I'm needing a new stable lad at this very moment.'

So Iain found service in the stables of the King of Eirinn, and sure enough, among the horses entrusted to his care was the Yellow Bay Filly that the Big Women of

Dhiurradh desired to have for their own. After a little while, Iain decided that the time had come for him to make good his escape; and one night, when everyone was asleep, he crept down to the stable and untethered the Yellow Bay Filly. Never forgetting the Fox's warning, he led the horse carefully to the stable door, preparing to mount and flee away. But alas! Just as he was going through the doorway, one hair of the filly's tail brushed against the gate-post, which immediately sent forth a screech that could have been heard throughout the length and breadth of Eirinn.

At once all the royal household came running out to the stable, with the King himself at their head.

'You are trying to steal my Yellow Bay Filly from me!' he shouted in anger. 'You are fleeing with that which is not yours!'

'Forgive me!' cried Iain, 'but it was the Big Women of Dhiurradh who sent me out to seek it for them. For until I take the filly to them, they will not give me their White Sword of Light; and until I give the White Sword of Light to the Giant of the Five Heads, the Five Humps, and the Five Throttles, he will not let me have his blue falcon. And without the blue falcon I may not return home to my stepmother the Queen.'

Then the King of Eirinn looked at Iain with a guileful expression.

'I will give you my Yellow Bay Filly,' he said, 'if you can bring me the daughter of the King of France. For I have heard that she is the most beautiful woman in the world, and I want to marry her.'

And when Iain had promised to carry out the King's wish and had set off with a joyful countenance, the King of Eirinn laughed until tears fell from his eyes. For he thought that Iain Direach would never be able to succeed in the task he had set him.

When he reached the shore, Iain found the Fox waiting there as he had promised.

'Och, never tell me you have failed to bring away the Yellow Bay Filly from the King of Eirinn's stable,' he greeted Iain.

'Alas, it is so,' replied Iain; and he told the Fox that the Yellow Bay Filly would not be his until he had fetched to Eirinn the daughter of the King of France.

Then the Fox looked at Iain with the cunning wisdom of his kind and said:

'Your task is hard, but if you are careful it should not be impossible. I will grow into a ship and take you over to France, which lies farther yet over the ocean. And when we reach France you must go to the King's house and ask for help, saying that your ship lies wrecked upon the shore. Then the King and Queen and their daughter will come out to see your ship; and if you leave future events to me, all will be well.'

And straightway the Fox turned into a handsome ship with pointed bows, and carried Iain over the water to France. As soon as they landed upon the shore, Iain set off for the King's house, and when he knocked at the great door it was opened by the King of France himself.

'What do you want of me, stranger?' asked the King, and he a fine gentleman with a black beard.

'Oh sire, my ship lies wrecked close by the shore,' said Iain, 'and I have come to seek your help.'

'I will come and see your ship,' said the King; and then he called for his wife and daughter to accompany him to the shore.

Now when Iain Direach beheld the daughter of the King of France, he thought she was the loveliest creature he had ever set eyes on, and knew that the King of Eirinn had been right when he said that she was the most beautiful woman in the world. She had long, dark hair and deep blue eyes, and there was great gentleness in her face.

The three of them went down to the shore with Iain, and when they saw his ship they exclaimed at its great size. And while Iain stood there wondering what he should do next, suddenly he heard the sound of sweet music coming from his vessel. The King's daughter heard it also, and she clapped her hands in delight.

' Will you not take me on your ship that I may see the musicians ? ' she asked Iain.

' Gladly,' replied Iain; and while the King and Queen stood smiling by, he took her white hand and led her on board. And while they were exploring the rich cabins below, the sails filled with a homing wind and the ship set off across the ocean, so that when Iain and the Princess came on deck again, they found themselves in the middle of the sea, with never a piece of land in sight.

' Alas, you have stolen me away from my mother and father ! ' cried the Princess.

' Forgive me,' Iain answered her. ' But it was the King of Eirinn who sent me forth to bring you across the sea to be his wife '—and he told her the whole tale of his adventures, and how he might not return home to his stepmother the Queen without the blue falcon that belonged to the Giant of the Five Heads, the Five Humps, and the Five Throttles.

And when he had finished, the Princess sighed and gazed fondly upon him with her deep blue eyes.

' Noble Iain, I would rather marry you than a hundred Kings of Eirinn,' she said. And Iain was sorrowful at her words, because a great love had sprung up in his heart for the Princess, and the thought that he must part from her was heavy.

But once more the faithful Fox helped him in his trouble. No sooner had they landed upon the green shore of Eirinn than he regained his own shape and told Iain how he might outwit the King of Eirinn and keep the Princess for himself.

'I will change into the form of a fine woman,' he said, 'and while the Princess stays here on the shore, you must take me to the King and pretend I am the daughter of the King of France.' And he added with a crafty smile: 'I will devise my own escape and rejoin you later.'

So it was that while the Princess stayed by the shore, Iain set off through the green countryside with the Fox walking beside him in the guise of a fine woman with a pale, pointed face and curling, red-brown hair. They came to the royal palace, and were received by the King himself, who was amazed indeed to see his stable lad again.

'Ho, King of Eirinn,' said Iain, 'I have brought you the daughter of the King of France to be your bride. Where is the Yellow Bay Filly that you promised to give me when I had fulfilled my mission?'

'You have done well,' replied the King; and he ordered the Yellow Bay Filly to be made ready with a golden saddle and a silver bridle, and led forth from the stable.

'Take my Yellow Bay Filly,' he said to Iain, 'and go on your way.'

Then Iain rode off on the Yellow Bay Filly to the shore where the Princess waited. The King of Eirinn, meanwhile, turned to embrace his bride; but he had no sooner clasped her in his arms than she was suddenly transformed into a red-brown beast who bit him to the bone and then ran swiftly away to the shore. There the Fox transformed himself once more into a bark with red-brown sails, and sailed with Iain and the Princess and the Yellow Bay Filly across the water to the Island of Dhiurradh.

'And now,' he told Iain when they had landed there,

' I will tell you how to outwit the three Big Women and keep the Yellow Bay Filly for yourself. I will change into the likeness of a fine horse, and while the Princess stays here on the shore with the Filly, you must take me to the Big Women and pretend I am that which they sent you to find.' And once again he added with a cunning smile: ' I will devise my own escape and join you later.'

So it was that while the Princess and the Yellow Bay Filly stayed on the shore under the craggy cliffs, Iain set off for the house of the Big Women with the Fox walking beside him in the shape of a fine horse. They were astonished indeed to see him return.

' Ho, sisters,' said Iain. ' I have brought you the Yellow Bay Filly of the King of Eirinn as you asked me to do. Where is the White Sword of Light that you promised to give me when I had fulfilled my task ? '

' You have done well, king's son,' said the Big Women; and she who was as tall as a fir-tree lifted the sword from its place and delivered it into his hands.

' Take our White Sword of Light,' they said, ' and go on your way.'

Then Iain set off for the shore again, brandishing the magnificent weapon as he went and feeling its supple blade quiver in his grasp. Left by themselves, the three Big Women were all eagerness to try out their new steed; and because none of them would let the other be the first to ride it round about, all three of them mounted the filly at once, one on top of the other's shoulders. The Fox no sooner felt them perched on his back than he kicked up his heels and galloped off to the very edge of the cliffs. And there he dug his hooves into the turf and lowered his head, so that all together the three Big Women—the tall one, the dark one, and the ugly one—were pitched headlong into the sea below, where they remain to this day.

K

Then, having regained his proper shape, the Fox rejoined those who were waiting for him on the shore, and as a narrow red-brown boat he carried them across the water and back to the land from which Iain Direach had first set out.

' And now that our sea-faring days are over,' said the Fox, ' I will tell you how to outwit the Giant of the Five Heads, the Five Humps, and the Five Throttles, and keep the White Sword of Light for yourself. I will change myself into the likeness of a bright weapon, and while the Princess remains here with the Yellow Bay Filly and the White Sword of Light, you must take me to the Giant and pretend I am that which he sent you to find.'

And yet again he added with his guileful smile: ' I will devise my own escape and join you later.'

So it was that while the Princess remained on the shore with the Filly and the Sword of Light, Iain set off for the Giant's house, carrying the Fox in the shape of a shining weapon. The Giant was indeed astounded to see him again.

' Ho, Giant,' said Iain, ' I have brought you the White Sword of Light from the Big Women of Dhiurradh, as you bade me. Where is the blue falcon that you promised to give me when I had fulfilled my task ? '

' You have done well, king's son,' said the Giant; and he fetched the blue falcon and placed it in a wicker basket and gave it to Iain. ' Take my blue falcon,' he said, ' and go on your way.'

Then Iain went off to rejoin the Princess where she waited on the shore. And as he saw the blink of blue wings between the wicker-work of the basket, there was joy in his heart beyond all measure to think that at last he had secured the marvellous bird on whose account he had first embarked on all his adventures.

Now as soon as he was left alone with his new sword in

his hand, the Giant could not wait to know the feel and the strength of it. He began fencing with an imaginary assailant, slashing the air and thrusting to right and left with the sharp-edged blade—until the Fox suddenly bent himself in the air and cut off the Giant's five heads in one mighty sweep. Then he threw off the last of his disguises and ran to rejoin Iain and the Princess.

' And now,' said the Fox, ' your adventures are almost at an end. It only remains for you to overcome the bad magic of your stepmother the Queen. And the way that shall be done is this. You must mount the Yellow Bay Filly and take up the Princess behind you. In your right hand you must hold the White Sword of Light with the flat of the blade turned towards your nose, while the blue falcon perches upon your shoulder. In this fashion you must set off for your home, and by and by you will meet your stepmother along the road. She will try to bewitch you with a deadly glance that would make you fall from the filly transformed into a faggot of dry sticks; but because the sharp edge of the sword will be turned towards her, her bad magic will not prevail.'

So according to the Fox's bidding Iain set off for his his home, with the Princess mounted behind him on the Yellow Bay Filly, the White Sword of Light held with the flat of the blade turned to his nose, and the blue falcon perched on his shoulder. And after journeying over more valleys and hills than could be counted by a knowledgeable man, he reached the outskirts of his father's palace at last.

Now the Queen happened to be looking from her window as Iain rode over the hill; and with black wickedness against her stepson in her heart, she hurried out beyond the courtyard gates to meet him as he came. And as he drew near, she bent upon him a glance so deadly that had the White Sword of Light not been held before him, he would surely have fallen from his steed as the Fox had prophesied. But because the sharp edge of that bright sword was towards his stepmother, all her bad magic was turned upon herself, and it was she who fell to the ground as a faggot of dry sticks.

Then Iain entered his father's house in triumph, leading his Princess by the hand; and when the King learnt the full story of his son's adventures, he prepared a splendid marriage feast for the two of them, and ordered that the bundle of sticks that lay beyond the courtyard gates should be burnt upon the fire.

And this was the manner in which Iain Direach settled down to enjoy prosperity and happiness for the rest of his life. He had the most beautiful woman in the world as his wife; in his stable was the Yellow Bay Filly, the swiftest horse that ever lived, who could leave one wind behind and catch the next that lay before it; hanging on the wall of his house was the invincible White Sword of Light; and for his hunting he had the blue falcon, whose prowess was unmatched by any other bird.

He did not forget that it was to his old friend the Fox that he owed the happiness of these possessions, and he told *An Gille Mairtean* that so long as he lived, neither he nor any of his kind would be molested in their hunting. But in reply, the Fox just smiled at Iain.

'Don't you be bothering yourself about me or my kind,' he said. 'For we are well able to look after ourselves.' And away he went over the hill-side, with his red brush held proudly behind him.

And so the tale is spent.

The Three Sons of Gorla

GORLA the goatherd and his wife lived in a little shieling on *Beinne-nan-Sian*, which is the Hill of Storms. They had a yellow-haired daughter and three handsome sons: Black Ardan, the proud one; Red Ruais, the long-winded one; and Brown Caomhan, the gentle one.

One day when the daughter was out herding the young kids on the breast of the hill, a thick white mist of enchantment came down upon her, and when it rose again she had vanished utterly. Then there was sad sorrow in the shieling on the Hill of Storms; and when a day and a year had passed, and still she had not returned, Black Ardan rose up and said:

' I will go forth from my father's house, and I will not rest by day or night until I find my sister.'

Then Gorla his father said quietly: ' I will not hinder thy going, my son. But it would have become thee better, before the word went from thy mouth, to ask thy father's leave.'

Ardan only shrugged his shoulders at this; and then

137

his mother rose up, and she baked a big bannock and a little bannock.

'Now, my son,' she said, 'dost thou prefer to take with thee on thy journey the big bannock with thy mother's anger, because thou didst not ask leave to go from thy father's house, or the little bannock with her blessing?'

'For me,' answered Ardan, 'the big bannock. Keep the little bannock and thy blessing for those that choose them.'

And with the big bannock in his pouch, he set off on his quest. Swiftly he travelled through the countryside. He sent splashes from every pool, and dust from the top of every hillock, sparing neither sole nor instep until he reached the Wood of the Roedeer. Here hunger seized him, and he sat down upon a flat grey stone to eat his bannock. But before his teeth had sunk into it, there was a flap of wings and a black raven flew from the wood and perched on a snout of rock above his head.

'A morsel, a morsel, son of Gorla of the Flocks!' he cried.

'Not a morsel shalt thou get from me, thou hideous, stare-blind creature,' said Ardan. 'It is little enough I have for myself.'

And taking no further notice of the Raven, he finished his bannock to the last crumb.

Then he continued on his way; and as he journeyed the dark clouds of night descended on the earth. And coming over the crest of one hill-side, he saw before him a little house of light, where he thought he would seek shelter. When he reached the house, the door was opened by an old, wrinkled man who gave him a good welcome.

'Often has my bright light attracted the traveller of the hills,' said the Old Man.

When Ardan had supped and rested, the Old Man asked him whether he would be willing to take service with him.

'I am wanting a herd for my three dun-polled cows,' he said.

Ardan told him that he was journeying to seek his sister, but said: 'Yet I will stay by the way and take service with thee if the reward thou offerest is great enough.'

'Thou shalt get thy reward,' the Old Man told him, 'and there will not be cause for complaining.'

So the next day Black Ardan rose up and prepared to set off into the hills with the three dun-polled cows. Before he went, the Old Man said to him:

'Promise me that thou wilt not try to lead the cows, or goad them on, but follow behind them and let them seek their own pasture. And whatever happens, give me thy word that thou wilt not stray from their side.'

Thinking to himself that this was easy herding, Ardan gave his promise to the Old Man, and departed from his house with a light step, following the cows as they led him over two hills and into a green glen. Now as he went on through the glen, Ardan suddenly saw a strange sight: a golden cock and a silver hen flew out of the sky and went running on before him. O, but the cock's tail feathers glittered yellow in the sun, and the breast of the hen shone silver-bright; and Ardan at once forgot his promise to the Old Man, and started running after them. His feet sped over the green grass, and his hand all but grasped one of those glittering tail feathers when behold! cock and hen vanished into the air, and there was no more sight of them.

Cursing himself for his folly, Ardan returned to the three cows, who were grazing the grass of the glen. And then he rubbed his eyes in amazement: for jumping along before him was a rod of gold and a rod of silver.

' There is enough gold and silver to keep me in
wealth for the rest of my days ! ' he thought; and forthwith he set off after them.   But before he had taken eight
paces, behold! golden rod and silver rod vanished entirely.

Once more he returned to the three dun-polled cows,
determined not to be caught out a third time.   And
leaving their grazing, the cows moved on along the glen.
Ardan followed close after them until they passed the
end of the glen, where he gasped in astonishment.   For
there grew a grove of trees that bore every fruit he had
ever seen in his life, and twelve kinds that he had not.
Their boughs were bent to the ground under the weight
of them, bright-skinned and summer-ripe; and straightway Ardan entered the grove and gorged himself until
he could eat no more.

When he returned to the cows, they at once turned
round and set off on their homeward way; and soon they
were back at the Old Man's house.

' Now I will milk my three dun-polled cows,' said the
Old Man; ' and that way I shall discover whether thou
hast been a faithful herd to me, and kept the promise thou
didst make.'

But from the udders of the three cows streamed milk
that was thin and poor; and by this the Old Man knew
that Ardan had not kept faith, but had strayed from the
side of the cows.

' Young man without truth and without faithfulness ! '
he cried.   ' This is the reward of thy herding——'

He slowly raised his hand; and where he stood, Black
Ardan was turned into a pillar of stone.

.   .   .   .   .

A day and a year passed; and in the shieling on the Hill
of Storms, Red Ruais, the second son of Gorla the herd,
rose up and said:

' I will go forth from my father's house, and I will not

rest by day or night until I find my sister and Ardan my brother.'

Then it happened as before, that Gorla rebuked his son for not asking leave of him; and at this, Ruais merely spread wide his hands in a gesture of contempt. And when his mother asked him whether he would take with him the big bannock and her anger, or the little bannock with her blessing, he replied as Ardan had done before him:

' For me the big bannock. Keep the little bannock and thy blessing for those that choose them.'

Then he set off; and exactly as it happened to Black Ardan, the eldest son of Gorla the herd, so it happened to the middle son. Red Ruais met the Black Raven in the Wood of the Roedeer, and he refused him a morsel of of his bannock. He came to the house of the Old Man, and set out to herd the three dun-polled cows. He broke his promise and pursued the gold cock and the silver hen, and the golden rod and the silver rod; and he ate of the fruits that grew in the grove at the end of the green glen. And when he returned to the Old Man's house, he was turned into a pillar of stone, and the two brothers stood side by side as a token of broken troth.

And after another day and a year, Gorla's youngest son, Brown Caomhan, rose up and said:

' There are now three days and three years since our sister vanished; and though both my brothers have departed to seek her, we have heard no word from them. Now, father, if it is pleasing to thee, allow me to go after them and share their fate.'

' Thou hast my leave and my blessing, Caomhan,' replied his father.

Then his mother said: ' Shall I prepare for thee the big bannock without my blessing, or the little bannock with the goodwill of my heart ? '

' Thy blessing, oh mother, give thou to me,' replied Caomhan. ' Poor to me would be the inheritance of the great world itself, if thy blessing were not at its foot.'

Then his parents wished upon him the soft path for the far traveller, and he set off upon his journey. He went as the wind through the land; the mossy places trembled as he drew near them, the dew fell from the bushy purple heather when he trod upon the hill-side; and the red grouse fled at his coming. When he reached the Wood of the Roedeer, he sat down upon the flat grey stone to eat his bannock; and out from the trees flew the Black Raven.

' A morsel, a morsel, son of Gorla of the Flocks ! ' he cried.

' Thou shalt get a morsel, poor creature,' Caomhan replied. ' It is likely that thou art needier than I. It will suffice for both of us, for the blessing of a mother is at its foot.'

Then he broke the little bannock in two pieces and gave half to the Raven, who flew off carrying it in his beak.

Night came, and in the darkness Caomhan saw the house of light before him. The Old Man bade him

welcome, and after he had supped and rested, he asked Caomhan, as he had asked his two brothers before him, whether he would be willing to herd his three dun-polled cows for him.

' I am engaged on a quest for the sister of my affection and the brothers of my love,'

Caomhan answered. ' But if thou art in need of a herd, then I will stay and help thee for a while, Old Man. For I can see that because of thy great age, thou thyself cannot go out upon the hill-side.'

So in the morning Caomhan prepared to set out with the three cows, and before he left he promised the Old Man that he would let them seek their own pasture, and that whatever happened, he would not stray from their side. Over two hills he followed them until they reached the green glen; and here the gold cock and the silver hen flew out of the sky and ran before him. Yet for all the glitter and shine of them, Caomhan remembered his promise and stayed close by the three cows.

And as they continued on their way, the rod of gold and the rod of silver came jumping before his eyes. But still he remained a steadfast herd, although he had never imagined to see such wealth in all his life. At the end of the glen the cows led him close to the grove of fruit-trees; and though their bright skins and the sun-ripe smell of them made his mouth run with water, he passed by without a lingering step.

Suddenly the air was full of smoke, and there was a smell of burning all around; and Caomhan saw that they were approaching a wide moor where the heather was all alight. Angry flames rolled across it like swollen storm-waves of the sea; and yet the three cows went onward just the same. And remembering his promise not to leave their side in spite of all that might happen, Coamhan followed them over that burning moor, though the knees of him trembled with fear. But he and the three cows came through the heather in perfect safety: not a hair of them was burnt, and the sole of his foot remained unscorched.

In a little while the roar of rushing waters reached his ears; and soon he saw before him a swollen river, yellow and swirling. It was so deep that had many men stood upon each other's shoulders, yet their nostrils would have filled with water. To his dismay, the three cows stepped calmly off the river-bank into the midst of the waters; and though the teeth of him chattered with fright, Caomhan remembered his promise and followed them. And in a few moments they were all standing on the opposite bank dry and unharmed, having passed through the raging waters without peril.

Forthwith the cattle turned homeward by another route; and before long they were back at the Old Man's house.

'Now I will milk my three cows,' said he, 'and that way I shall discover whether thou hast been a faithful herd to me.'

From the udders of the three cows poured forth milk that was creamy and rich: and by this the Old Man knew that Caomhan had kept faith.

'Thou art a true herd,' he said. 'Hadst thou not observed thy promise to me, it would have fared with thee as with thy two faithless brothers'—and drawing Caomhan into another room, he showed him Black Ardan and Red Ruais, who stood there stone-still. A terrible pity entered Caomhan's heart at this sight, and he perceived that the Old Man was one who had the power of magic.

'Doubtless it was also he who spirited away my yellow-haired sister,' he thought.

'Come, Caomhan,' said the Old Man, 'demand of me the reward of thy herding. Whatever thou ask, that shalt thou get.'

'Restore to me, alive and well as when they left my father's house, the brothers of my love,' said Caomhan. 'And if it is in thy power, restore also the sister of my affection.'

At these words the Old Man frowned, and was displeased.   Yet he could not go back on his word entirely; and so he said:

' Youth, thy request is high.   Before I grant it to thee, there are three things thou must do.'

' Name them,' said Caomhan.

' Listen then.   From the high mountain yonder thou must bring to me the swift roe-deer.   Dappled is her side, slender her foot, magnificent her antlers.   This is the first of thy tasks.

' From the deep loch near by thou must fetch for me the green duck with the yellow neck.   This is the second of thy tasks.

' And from the dark rocky pool on the hill-side thou must get me the white-bellied, red-gilled trout with the silver tail.   This is the third and last of thy tasks.'

Then away went Brown Caomhan to the high mountain, to embark on the first of his tasks without delay. Proud on a crag he saw the slender-footed roe-deer, and immediately set off in purusit of her.   But though his speed was so great that the sole of his foot scarcely stirred the springy turf, he could not draw near her. When he was on one hillock, she would be five hillocks farther from him.

' O ! ' cried Caomhan, ' that I had the fleet heels of a hunting dog ! '

No sooner had the words gone from his mouth than there was a bounding by his side, and there crouched a panting hound eager for the chase.

' The Black Raven has commanded me to overtake the slender doe-deer for thee, Caomhan,' said the hound, ' because thou didst divide thy bannock with him.'

And away he sped, to return in a little moment and lay the dappled-sided roe-deer at Caomhan's feet.   Then Caomhan slung the deer across his shoulder-blades and betook himself to the deep loch where lived the green duck with the yellow neck.   She was flying high above his head; and seeing her so far beyond his reach, he cried:

'O! that I had the strong wings and sharp eye of a bird!'

And immediately the Black Raven himself came out of the sky.

'I will bring down the green duck for thee, Caomhan,' he said, 'because thou didst show kindness to me.'

Away he soared, and the next instant the yellow-necked duck was stretched on the ground before Caomhan.   Then, with the roe-deer on his back and holding the duck by its neck, he went on to the rocky pool on the hill-side, where swam the white-bellied, red-gilled trout with the silver tail.   Sly-still he lay under a flat stone; and with all his skill of fishing, Caomhan could not catch him.

'O! that I was like the otter!' he cried, 'who swims the stream and dives under the wave.'

Straightway, what should appear by his side but a smooth brown otter who said: 'The Black Raven has commanded me to get for thee the red-gilled trout, Caomhan, because thou took pity on his hunger.'

The otter dived into the pool, and in one swift movement he took the trout from behind the stone, and delivered it up to Caomhan.

And bearing the roe-deer, the green duck, and the silver-tailed trout, Caomhan returned in triumph to the house of the Old Man.

'I have accomplished the three tasks which thou didst set me,' he told the Old Man.   'According to thy promise, restore to me now the brothers of my love and the sister of my affection.'

The Old Man marvelled to see the trophies Caomhan brought to him.

' Oh, my son,' he said, ' well art thou named *Caomhan*, the noble one, the gentle one. According to my promise I will restore to thee the brothers of thy love and the sister of thy affection, whom I have kept under enchantment since she vanished from the misty hill.'

And forthwith Black Ardan and Red Ruais put on their flesh once more, and the blood again ran through their veins. They embraced Caomhan with tenderness; and never more did they show pride or arrogance so long as they lived. But greater yet was the three brothers' rejoicing when their sister of the yellow hair appeared before them, alive and well.

At once they rose up and set off for the house of their father, Gorla the goatherd; and as they departed, the Old Man stood at his door and called after them: ' Fare thee well! May the blessing of Age be on thy journeying and on thy going ! '

And that day there was joy and laughter in the little shieling on *Beinne-nan-Sian*, the Hill of Storms.

The Ailp King's Children

THERE was a battle long ago under frozen hills and sombre trees, between the Ailp King and the Druids. And when the fighting was done, the Ailp King and all his followers lay dead upon the ground, while the Druids sang wild songs of triumph, marching through his palace. In the shadow of the great doorway there, they found the Ailp King's children crouching: a boy and girl, who were dragged before the victors with joyful shouts.

'We will take the girl-child to dwell with us,' they declared; and to show that she belonged to them, a woman of the Druids stepped forward and touched her fair flesh, which immediately became as green as grass.

But before they could decide what they should do with the Ailp King's son, he tore himself from his captors' grasp and fled away from that place with the swiftness of a stag that is pursued, never resting the sole of his foot until he reached the top of the mountain called *Beinn ghloine*, which is the Hill of Glass. Yet as he slept upon its icy pinnacle that night, a Druid came after him and invoked an evil spell upon his straight young limbs, so that he was changed into a greyhound, keeping only the use of his human tongue, and was forced to follow his enemy back to the palace. There the Druids sent the Ailp princess to look after her brother, for she refused to listen to the teachings of their womenfolk, and they were well pleased to be rid of her.

' The green girl-child and the greyhound shall dwell together in their father's house,' decreed the Arch-Druid. ' And they shall not break the strong spell of their enchantment until two things come to pass.

' When a woman shall consent of her own accord to stay with the greyhound for the rest of her life, then the Prince shall regain his rightful shape. And when the Princess is kissed by a king's son, then her flesh will become as fair as it was before.'

Then, as the Princess stood in the palace doorway, with one green arm encircling the greyhound's neck, the Arch-Druid swept his arm in a wide gesture around the courtyard, which was littered with the bones of those who had fallen in the great battle. And before he departed from that place for ever, he uttered one more prophecy.

' The bones of your father and his followers shall remain unburied, bleached white by the sun and washed smooth by the rain, until the children of your children give them a resting-place,' he said.

For many years brother and sister lived alone in their father's house. And while the sea of bracken without their gates grew higher round about them, the days of their childhood passed away. Tall and straight, the green-skinned Princess would wander through the deserted rooms, her green hair falling on her shoulders; and at her heels would follow the slim greyhound with his human eyes and power of speech, and in his mind the long thoughts of youth.

L

Now at this time the King of Urbhih, who dwelt near by, set off with three hundred men to fight a distant foe. But he had barely begun his march through the hills when a thick white mist came down from the sky, and his feet strayed from their path. Dismayed, the King groped onwards, vainly trying to regain his way and discern his followers.

'Keep with me!' he cried; but from the impenetrable obscurity round about there answered but a hundred men.

Yet still the King continued onward, and when he caught the faint gleam of a quiet tarn upon his right hand, he cried again:

'Keep with me!'

And this time there answered but twenty of his followers.

Drawing his claymore as if he would slash the mist away, the King again went forward. And when he discerned the faint outline of a mighty fir-tree upon his left hand, he cried for the third time:

'Keep with me!'

And there answered him but three of all his army.

At last he stopped, knee-high in gnarls of bracken, and called upon his men for the last time. But now no answering call came to his cry, and he knew that he was utterly alone.

Claymore in hand, he stayed where he was, until at last the mist rolled away from the hills, shredding into scraps of cloud across a blue sky. And where should he be but in the shadow of the Ailp King's house, whose neglected walls, breached by the invading bracken, stood immediately before him. Cautiously the King of Urbhih passed through the unguarded gateway, to find himself in that deserted courtyard yet littered with the bones of the long battle-fallen, bleached white by the sun and washed smooth by the rain. Wondering what bitter strife had caused this scene of desolation, he crossed the courtyard to enter the house; and as he went, his foot struck the skull of the Ailp King himself, so that it rolled from one end of the courtyard to the other.

All at once, a fierce greyhound rushed out from the great door of the house, and leapt upon the King in savage fury. But the King's dismay at this sudden attack was less than his astonishment at hearing a young man's voice issue from the beast as it pinioned him to the ground, its teeth at his throat.

'You have desecrated the bones of my father,' it snarled. 'You have trespassed among those who must remain unburied until they are taken up by our children's children.'

'Spare my life!' pleaded the King of Urbhih in terror. 'Whoever you may be, hound with a human tongue, spare my life!'

At that moment a clear voice called from the house.

'Spare the life of the stranger, my brother. For who can tell? He may be able to deliver us from our enchantment.'

The greyhound leapt to one side; and as he rose shakily to his feet, the King saw a slender girl whose skin and hair were coloured a brilliant green, coming towards him across the courtyard.

'What place is this?' he demanded in fear. 'And who are you, uncanny beings?'

'This is the house of the Ailp King, who was killed in battle with our enemies, the Druids,' replied the Princess. 'And we are the Ailp King's hapless children.'

Then the greyhound stepped forward.

'What is your name, stranger?' he asked.

'I am the King of Urbhih. And I have left behind me a son and a daughter who will mourn for me all the days of their life if I do not return to them.'

Now at this reply, a cunning plan entered the head of the Ailp King's son, and he drew his sister aside and spoke privately to her, explaining what was in his mind.

'We must contrive to get the daughter of this King within our house,' he said, 'for then I may hope to prevail upon her to stay with me for the rest of her life, and the evil spell that lies upon me will be broken. And who knows? It may well be that her brother will also release you from your unhappy enchantment, bestowing upon you the kiss of a king's son.'

'These are joyful thoughts,' answered his sister. 'But how shall we accomplish your plan? For since the woman must agree to stay with you without knowing that you are in truth a prince; and since the King's son must desire to kiss me without knowing that I am the victim of the Druids' magic, we may not disclose the secret of our enchantment to the King of Urbhih—who, if he did but learn it, would surely hasten to deliver us from our unhappiness without delay.'

'True, sister,' said the Prince. 'Therefore we must tell the King that we will spare his life for a year only, so that he may return to his kingdom and make preparations for his son to succeed him. And you must accompany him when he goes hence, and bring back his daughter as a hostage to ensure that he will return when twelve months are ended.

'Thus we shall bring the King's daughter to our house —and the rest will depend upon ourselves. If we do not succeed in our task, then we may look to remain in luckless solitude for the rest of our days.'

They told the King their plan, and with sorrow in his heart he promised to abide by it. Then he and the Ailp King's daughter set off together across the trackless waste of bracken, and never rested by light or dark until they reached his palace.

And it was not long before the greyhound waiting by the gateway saw his sister returning across the hill-side, accompanied by a young princess too proud to show her fear. She was Oighrig, the daughter of the King of Urbhih, and as soon as he set eyes on her, the Ailp King's son knew he would never see a lovelier maiden in the world. She was welcomed into the house with all the courtesy and honour that its vanished splendour could afford; and soon her hatred and distrust of her strange guardians changed to mere bewilderment. She could not understand why the greyhound of the gentle eyes and the green girl of the kindly speech should desire her father's death. But in vain she pleaded with them to spare his life.

'There is some secret you are keeping from me,' she cried at last; 'for I know there is no cruelty in your hearts.'

Harebells nodded in the April weather; lapwings wheeled against the summer sky; in the autumn scarlet berries hung in clusters from the mountain ash: and now the time was near when the King of Urbhih must return to the Ailp King's children.

'How pleasant it is here in the midst of the hills!' Oighrig cried one autumn day; but though the greyhound's heart leapt with gladness, she did not speak the words he longed to hear.

When the first snow came down from the sky, he said to her:

'You will soon be leaving us, Princess; for tomorrow your father will return here, and you must go back to your own people.'

'Alone!' Oighrig cried in sorrow. 'Oh, do not let me return alone. I implore you yet once more to spare my father's life.'

Then she said quietly: 'Or, if you will not let us go

from this place together, then send away my father, and keep me to stay with you for ever, or kill me instead, as you will.'

The greyhound and the Ailp King's daughter gazed upon her with incredulous joy.

' You are really willing to stay here for the rest of your life ? ' they asked.

' Yes,' she replied, ' to save my father's life.'

Upon the instant that she spoke these words, a miraculous change overcame the Ailp King's son, for the power of the Druid's enchantment crumbled away, his hound's likeness fell from him, and he stood there in his own form, as a young man of princely bearing.

' Do not fear for your father,' he told Oighrig, smiling. ' For it was never in my heart to kill him.'

And then he told her the secret of his enchantment, while his sister clasped them both in her green arms, and wept for joy.

In the midst of their rejoicing the King of Urbhih entered the house and stood amazed at the sight which met his eyes. And presently, when he had learnt all the secret of the greyhound's enchantment, he departed home again to bring his son to the wedding-feast of Oighrig and the Ailp King's son: for they were to be married without delay.

At noon the next day the King of Urbhih and his son came riding over the hill-side, both of them mounted on swift-footed fillies. They were welcomed with glad greeting; and yet the Ailp King's daughter knew sorrow at the meeting, for the young Prince of Urbhih shrank back at the sight of her green skin and long green hair, while she herself felt a great love for him spring to her heart.

' Alas, I shall never win a kiss from him, and may look to spend the rest of my life under the Druids' spell,' she told her brother, with the tears falling down her green cheeks.

'Do not despair utterly,' he replied, 'but fetch a beaker full of the *mheadair Bhuidne*, or yellow mead, that is made from the wild bees' honey. In the old time it was said that this mead held magic properties: and who knows? It may well be the means to incline the Prince's heart towards you.'

His sister followed his advice, and approached the King of Urbhih's son with a beaker of the sun-filled mead held before her.

'Will you not try its heather taste?' she asked him. 'It will remind you of the blessed warmth of summer.'

The Prince took the beaker from her hand and raised it to his lips. And behold, as soon as he tasted the honeyed drink, a strange magic fell upon his eyes, so that he saw the Princess in her own fair form; and it seemed to him that she was a woman beyond compare. Setting down the beaker, he took her in his arms and kissed her; and immediately the Druids' evil enchantment was undone, and the Ailp King's daughter was fair indeed.

That day there were two wedding-feasts instead of one; and while Oighrig and the Ailp King's son stayed in the house of his father, to dwell there in happiness for the rest of their days, the Prince of Urbhih and the Ailp King's daughter journeyed back with the King of Urbhih as man and wife. And they, too, found good fortune all their life.

And in time the third prophecy of the Druids was fulfilled, for their children's children took up from the courtyard of the Ailp King's house the bones of those who had fallen in battle long ago, and gave them their resting-place at last.

The Prince and the Giant's Daughter

LONG ago, in the days of the giants, there lived a
Prince of Tethertown who was called Iain. It
happened one day that when Iain was out hunting,
he came across a raven that was being attacked by a snake;
and seeing that the bird was in imminent danger of being
killed, he drew his sling and aimed a stone at the snake,
which fell in lifeless coils to the ground. Imagine
Iain's astonishment when, on the moment that the snake
fell dead, the raven was transformed into a handsome
youth with dark, glossy hair and black eyes, who faced
the prince with the light of gratitude in his glance.

'A thousand thanks, king's son, for thus releasing me
from the raven-spell that was upon me,' he said; and
he held out to Iain a sharp-cornered, cloth-covered
bundle. 'Take this bundle and go on your way,' he
continued. 'But remember this: do not open the
bundle until you are in the place where you would most
wish to dwell.'

And with these words he vanished over the crest of
the hill.

Iain turned on his homeward way, filled with curiosity

as to what the bundle contained. It was very heavy, and by the time he reached the dark, dense wood that stood a few miles from his home, he was glad to lay it aside for a bit and rest.

' Now surely,' he thought to himself, ' it would not be a very terrible thing for me to open the bundle and just give a quick glance at what is inside it.'

And so, unable to withold his curiosity any longer, he undid the bundle there and then. Immediately, there sprang up before his astonished eyes the very grandest castle he had ever seen. Its turrets reached to the topmost branches of the trees round about, and it was surrounded with pleasant gardens and green orchards.

But while Iain stood gazing upon it in admiration, he realized how foolish he had been to succumb to his curiosity.

' If only I had waited until I was in the fair green hollow that lies opposite my father's house ! ' he moaned. ' For that is the place where I would most wish to dwell. If only I could be putting the castle back into the bundle and carrying it there now ! '

At this moment the sound of a heavy tread shook the trees of the wood. Their branches quivered, the ground quaked, and a great giant with flaming red hair and a fiery beard came into view.

' Bad's the place where you have built your house, king's son ! ' he roared, ' for this is ground that belongs to me.'

' Alas, it is not here I would wish it to be,' replied Iain, ' but I cannot get it back into my bundle again.'

Then the Giant smiled into his fiery beard and said:

' What reward would you give me if I put your grand castle back into the bundle for you, king's son ? '

' What's the reward you would ask of me ? ' said Iain.

'Give me your first-born son when he is seven years old,' replied the Giant.

Now Iain had no wife and no sons, and thought nothing of the Giant's request.

'Och, is that all?' he said. 'You shall have him.'

And straightway the Giant replaced the castle, with all its pleasant gardens and green orchards, back in the bundle, and Iain set off for home once more.

As soon as he reached the fair green hollow opposite his father's house he opened the bundle once more, and there, in the place where he most wished to dwell, the castle sprang up exactly as before. This time, full of joy, Iain entered through the great doorway; and inside his new home the first thing he found was a lovely, bright-eyed woman who smiled on him and said:

'Advance, king's son. Everything is in order for you if you will marry me this very night.'

Iain was well content to have found this lovely woman to be his wife, and so they were married straightway, and dwelt together in their new castle in peace and happiness. And when the old King died, Iain became King of Tethertown in his stead. Soon a son was born to the new King and his Queen; but never a thought did Iain give to the rash promise he had made in the wood— until, at the end of a day and seven years, the trees in his green orchards quivered, the ground quaked, and the Giant approached the castle to claim his reward.

'What does that terrible man with the flaming hair and fiery beard want of us, dear husband?' asked the Queen, who was looking from a window.

'My sorrow, he has come to claim our first-born son and carry him away,' Iain replied. And sadly he told her of the incident that had taken place between the Giant and himself so long ago.

'Leave all to me,' said the Queen when she had

heard his tale. 'For I think I see a way out of this business.'

Meanwhile, the Giant's demands had been growing louder every moment, and Iain called out:

'My son will be with you presently. His mother is making him ready for the journey.'

Then the Queen called for the Cook's son to be brought before her. He was the same age as the young Prince, and she thought that she could easily deceive the Giant by sending him away instead of her own son. So she arrayed him in the Prince's garments, and handed him over to the Giant, who set off for home. He had not gone very far, however, when he decided to make sure that it was indeed the young Prince who was walking by his side. He plucked a stout hazel-rod from a nearby tree and handed it to the Cook's son, saying:

'If your father had that rod in his hands, what would he do with it?'

'Why,' answered the Cook's son, 'he would beat the dogs and the cats if they went near the King's meat.'

Then the Giant knew that *this* was not the King's son, and he turned back to the Castle in a terrible rage. When the King and Queen saw him coming back, they knew their ruse had failed; but still the Queen did not despair, but called for the Butler's son to be brought before her. He, also, was but seven years old; and while the Giant waited impatiently outside, the Queen arrayed him in the young Prince's garments and then sent him away in the place of her own son.

The Giant had gone but a little way when again he decided to make sure that it was indeed the young Prince who was walking by his side; so once more he handed over the hazel-rod, saying:

'If your father had that rod in his hands, what would he do with it?'

'Why,' answered the Butler's son, 'he would beat the dogs and the cats if they went near the King's bottles and glasses.'

Then the Giant knew that *this* was not the King's son, and as he turned back to the Castle his rage was twice as terrible.

'Give me your son!' he cried out in a voice that shook the topmost turrets of the castle. 'And if it is not your own son this time, the highest stone of your grand house will very soon become the lowest!'

Sadly the Queen called the young Prince, who was playing with his wee dog in the courtyard, and delivered him into the Giant's keeping; for she knew that she could not deceive the Giant a third time. And as soon as he beheld the lad's upright bearing and comeliness, the Giant had no doubt at all that *this* was indeed the King's son.

Together they journeyed the vast distance that lay between the King's castle and the Giant's home, which stood beside a dark loch. There the Prince was made welcome and received with kindness in the Giant's household; and as the years passed by, he grew up to be a strong, handsome youth.

.   .   .   .   .

Now it happened one day that as he returned to the Giant's house from a morning's hunting over the hillside, the Prince heard a sweet sound of singing; and peering up, he saw a beautiful maiden with red-gold hair looking out of a topmost window.

'Lovely maiden, who are you?' he asked, feeling a great love for her spring up in his heart.

'I am the Giant's youngest daughter,' she replied, 'and I've long admired you as you went about my father's house.'

Then the Prince confessed his love for her, and the

Giant's daughter told him that she could think of no greater joy than to become his wife.

'But listen carefully to what I am about to say,' she went on, 'for on it our future happiness depends. Tomorrow my father will offer you the choice of my two elder sisters in marriage. You must refuse them both and tell him it is his youngest daughter you wish to marry. At this he will be filled with a great anger; but leave future events to me, and everything will end well.'

Sure enough, on the next day the Giant called the Prince to him and offered him the choice of his two eldest daughters in marriage. And remembering to do as the maiden had instructed him, the Prince said to the Giant:

'It is your youngest daughter that I wish to marry.'

At these words the Giant was indeed filled with a great anger; for his youngest daughter was his greatest treasure, and he intended her to marry a mighty king who lived near by. Then he thought how he would repay the Prince for his daring request, and he smiled craftily into his red beard.

'Your wish is a bold one, king's son,' he said. 'My youngest daughter is a treasure not lightly to be won, and if you would marry her, you must accomplish three tasks that I shall set you. If you fail in any of these tasks, then you will lose not only my daughter, but your life as well. What do you say? Are you willing to risk your life to attain this whim of your heart?'

'Willingly,' answered the Prince. 'For life without this whim of my heart would be as worthless as an unkindled fire.'

The next day, before the Giant departed for his day's hunting, he told the Prince that his first task was to clean the great byre that stood in the courtyard. Filled with the dung of a hundred cattle, it had not been cleaned for seven years.

'And when I return this evening,' said the Giant, 'the byre must be so clean that a golden apple will run smoothly from one end of it to the other. If it is not so, then tonight your blood will quench my thirst.'

The Prince listened to his words with a great sinking of his heart. But nevertheless, he rose early the next morning and made his way to the byre to embark on this hopeless task. Now as soon as the Giant had left the house and departed over the hill-side, his youngest daughter came out to the Prince as he toiled to no avail, and told him not to despair.

'Did I not say that all would end well?' she said. 'Cease worrying, rest yourself in the shade of the great tree by the door, and go to sleep.'

The Prince, not without some misgiving, did as he was told, and soon fell into a deep sleep in the shade of the tree. It was nearly dusk when he awoke, and of the Giant's daughter there was no sign; and to his amazement he saw that the byre had been cleaned so thoroughly that a golden apple would have run smoothly from one end to the other.

Very shortly the Giant returned; and when he saw that the first of the Prince's tasks had been accomplished he drew his bristly red eyebrows together in a terrible frown.

'How it was done I do not know,' he said. 'And yet, since it is done, I must set you your second task.'

And he told the Prince that the next day he must thatch the byre with the plumage of a million birds, and that no two feathers must be of the same colour.

'And if this is not done by the time that I return this evening,' he said, 'then your blood will quench my thirst tonight.'

If it was early that the sun rose the next morning, it was earlier yet that the Prince set out for the moors, with

little hope in his heart and his bow and arrow in his hand
to shoot the birds and take their feathers for his task.
But ill luck attended him, and by midday he had only
secured two blackbirds, with feathers of the very same
hue.   Then the Giant's youngest daughter came to him
as he toiled to no avail, and told him not to despair.

' Did I not say that all would end well ? ' she said.
' Cease worrying, rest yourself on a bed of fragrant
heather, and go to sleep.'

The Prince did as he was told, thinking that he would
surely wake to a swift death; and he fell into a deep
sleep among the heather.   Darkness was coming over
the moors when he awoke, and of the Giant's daughter
there was no sign.   And when he made his way back to
the house, to his amazement he saw that the roof of the
byre shone with a million different hues, and was
thatched with the feathers of a million birds.

When the Giant found that the second task had been
completed, his rage was even greater than before.

' How it was done I do not know,' he said.   ' And
yet, since it is done, I must set you your third task.'

And he told the Prince that the next day his final task
must be to bring him for his supper the five magpie's eggs
that were in a nest at the top of the fir-tree by the loch.
And if he succeeded in this, then a grand wedding-feast
would be held that very night.

The next morning the Prince went down to the lochside as the water lay still in the early morning mist.   The
topmost branches of the fir-tree seemed to brush against
the clouds in the sky; and among them, far, far above his
head, he saw the little clotting in the foliage that was the
magpies' nest.   From the ground to the first branch of
that mighty tree there was a distance of five hundred
feet; and in vain the Prince tried to climb the scaly
trunk, tearing the flesh of his hands and tiring himself

uselessly. At midday, as he stood below the tree surveying his bleeding palms in despair, who should come to asist him in his trouble but the Giant's youngest daughter. But this time she did not bid the Prince rest and sleep.

Instead, she broke off her fingers one by one and stuck them in the side of the tree as hand- and foot-holds for the Prince. Away he went up the tree as fast as he could go, and at last, balanced perilously on a thin, swaying branch, he stretched forth his hand to take the magpies' nest.

'Oh, make haste, make haste!' cried the Giant's daughter from below, 'for my father is returning. His breath is burning my back!'

And such was the Prince's haste to reach the ground again that, although he got down with the five eggs safe and unbroken in their nest, he left the little finger from the maiden's left hand at the top of the tree.

'Now take the eggs and hasten with them to my father,' said the Giant's daughter. 'And tonight I shall be your wife if you can recognize me. For my father will array my two sisters and myself in garments that are exactly alike, with heavy veils over our faces. And after the wedding-feast is over, he will say to you: "Go to your wife, king's son"—and it is then that you must choose out of the three of us the one that is wanting the little finger of her left hand.'

Overjoyed to think that all his three tasks were accomplished, the Prince hastened to the Giant with the magpies' five eggs. Wrathful indeed was the Giant when he beheld them; yet he concealed his anger as best he might and bade a splendid wedding-feast to be set forth.

'Tonight the whim of your heart shall be satisfied, king's son,' he said; and added as he smiled his cunning smile into his red beard: 'If you can know your bride.'

And after the feast was over, when the heaped platters had been cleared of their meat and the overflowing vessels emptied of their ale, the Giant led the Prince to a little room where his three daughters were waiting. They were dressed exactly alike, in long gowns of snow-white wool; and heavy veils covered their faces, so that there could be no telling which was who.

'Now go to your wife, king's son,' sneered the Giant.

The Prince stepped towards the three women who stood before him, and without hesitation he took to him the one who was wanting the little finger of her left hand. When the Giant saw that in spite of all his schemes the Prince had won his youngest daughter from him, he was as angry as he had ever been; yet for the moment he could do nothing, and let him depart with his wife to the bridal chamber.

But as soon as the Prince and the Giant's daughter were alone together, she said to her husband:

'Now sleep not, lest you die. We must flee away before my father kills you.'

Then she took an apple and cut it into nine shares. Two shares she placed at the head of their bed; and two at the foot. As they went through the little door of the house she left two more shares there, and another two at the big door. And the last one she placed by the court-yard gate. Then they mounted the blue-grey filly that was tethered in the stable, and rode away on the wings of the wind.

Left in his house, the Giant presently called out to the couple, whom he imagined to be still in their chamber:

'Are you yet asleep?'

And the two shares of apple that were at the head of the bed replied: 'Not yet!'

After a little while the Giant called again, for he was

M

eager to come upon the Prince as he slept and slay him; and this time the two shares at the foot of the bed answered him: ' Not yet ! '

Yet a third time the two shares at the little door of the house spoke in reply; and as he heard the two that were at the big door, the Giant said, frowning:

' Now surely you are going farther away from me.'

It only remained for the piece of apple that was by the courtyard gate to answer him—and when he heard the faintness of its tone, the Giant sprang to his feet, exclaiming:

' You are fleeing from me ! '

He rushed out, and, filled with rage to discover how his daughter had tricked him, set off in hot pursuit of the two fugitives.

In the mouth of morning, when daylight first streaked across the sky, the Giant's daughter spoke up from her seat on the blue-grey filly and cried:

' Can you not hear the ground trembling ? It is my father that is almost upon us; his breath is burning my back ! '

' Alas, what can we do ? ' said the Prince. ' Is there any way to escape him yet ? '

' Put your hand into the ear of the blue-grey filly,' said the Giant's daughter, ' and whatever you find there, throw it behind you as you ride, so that it will fall in my father's path.'

The Prince did as he was told, and drew from the filly's ear a thorn-tree twig. And as soon as he cast it over his shoulder, behold! twenty miles of black thorn wood sprang up behind them, so dense and gnarled that scarcely a weasel could have crept through it. When the Giant saw this great obstacle in his path, he swore a mighty oath.

' Yet I will overtake them ! ' he roared, and turned

swiftly in his tracks to fetch his sharp-edged axe and wood knife. Returning, he made short work of hacking a way through that vast wood; and at midday, when the sun stood highest in the sky, the Giant's daughter again cried out:

'My father is almost upon us. His breath is burning my back!'

Once more she told the Prince to put his hand in the ear of the blue-grey filly and throw over his shoulder whatever he should find there. This time it was a small splinter of grey stone that he drew forth; and as soon as it touched the ground, behold! a barrier of craggy rock which was twenty miles long if it was twenty miles wide stretched out behind them.

'Yet I will overtake them! They shall not stop me!' swore the Giant when he saw this mountain in his way; and with earth-shaking strides he hurried away to fetch his strong lever and his mighty mattock. Darkness was falling by the time he had succeeded in cleaving his way through the rock; and as the moon was rising the Giant's daughter once more cried out:

'My father is almost upon us. His breath is burning my back!'

Without waiting to be told, the Prince put his hand into the ear of the blue-grey filly for the third time, and brought forth a tiny bladder of water. As soon as it had fallen over his shoulder, behold! a fathomless loch twenty miles long and twenty miles wide appeared behind them. The Giant, unable to slacken the furious pace of his pursuit, plunged headlong from the farther shore into the dark waters, and was drowned. And neither his daughter, nor the Prince, nor anyone else in the world ever saw him again.

Then the faithful blue-grey filly slowed into a steady trot under the light of the moon, and presently it seemed

to the Prince that he recognized the country round about.

'Surely we are nearing my father's house,' he said to his bride, 'for these are the fields where I played when I was a child.' And his heart filled with joy to think that he was returning home at last.

Soon they came to an old stone well, where they dismounted to rest for a while. And when the Prince rose up to resume his journey, the Giant's daughter said:

'It is best that you should go on alone to your father's house, to prepare him for my coming. I will wait here until you return.'

The Prince agreed to this; and as he rode off the Giant's daughter gave him a solemn warning:

'Dear heart,' she said, 'you must let no man nor beast kiss you while you are away; for if you do, a cruel oblivion will fall upon your brain, and you will forget me entirely.'

'Forget you!' echoed the Prince incredulously; but still he promised to observe his bride's strange warning.

So he rode on and came at last to his father's grand castle, that lay in the fair green hollow. And though he had been but seven years old when the Giant had claimed him, yet the Prince remembered well the high turrets, the pleasant gardens, and the green orchards that stood round about the castle. He left the blue-grey filly in the courtyard and strode into the great hall. His father and mother were seated at the high table, and as soon as they set eyes on the Prince's handsome countenance and upright bearing, they knew him for their son. They came forward and embraced him; but the Prince, remembering his warning, stopped them when they would have kissed his cheek. Filled with eagerness to fetch his bride, he had embarked upon the tale of his adventures when there was a sudden scuffling in the rushes under the table, and a slim grey hound hurled itself upon him with rapturous cries. It was the Prince's own wee dog, now fully grown.

But alas! Before the Prince could stop him, the hound had lavished kisses on him, and immediately all memory of the Giant's daughter vanished from his mind. And when his father prompted him to take up the thread of his story again, saying: ' You were telling us of a fair woman, my son . . .' the Prince gazed at him blankly and replied: ' What woman? There was no woman, my father.'

.   .   .   .   .

Meanwhile the Giant's daughter waited where the Prince had left her, by the well. And as the time went by and still he did not come, she guessed that what she had feared might happen had taken place, and that she was forgotten. Since there was no house within sight, she climbed into the branches of a tree that overhung the well, so that she would be safe from wolves, and decided to wait until someone might pass by.

She had no sooner settled herself in the fork of two boughs than footsteps sounded, and an old woman carrying a bucket approached the well. She was the wife of a shoemaker who lived near by, and he had sent her out to fill the bucket with water. She stooped over the well to let down her bucket, and then, to the wonder of the silent watcher in the tree above, she suddenly started back as though she had received a great shock. For mirrored in the surface of the water she had seen the beautiful image of the Giant's daughter—and being an ignorant and foolish old woman, she imagined it was her own reflection.

' Och, it's lovely to look upon I am!' she said, stroking her withered cheek. Then she went on: ' And why should the likes of me be made to carry water for a shambling, contemptible old carle like that old shoe-maker yonder?' And throwing down the bucket, she stumped off.

The poor shoemaker was amazed to see his wife come home in this manner, preening herself upon her ugliness; and, shrugging his shoulders, he set out to fetch the water himself. When he reached the well, the Giant's daughter called out to him from her tree, to ask where she might find shelter for the night; and as soon as he saw her lovely face, the shoemaker knew that it was her reflection that his wife had seen in the water. The end of that matter was happy, for the Giant's daughter went back to the shoemaker's house, and when the old wife realized what a foolish mistake she had made, she laughed herself out of all her proudness for ever. The old couple persuaded their guest to stay with them until she knew where it was she was wanting to go; and she meanwhile was always thinking how she might win back the Prince.

One day the old shoemaker came home in a state of

great excitement. ' For there's to be a grand wedding at the King's house,' he said, ' and there are new shoes to be made for the bridegroom and·all the household.'

When the Giant's daughter asked him who was the bridegroom, he answered: ' The young Prince himself is to marry the daughter of some rich lord.'

From then on, all the talk of the countryside was of the splendid marriage that was to be held in the King's house; and when the wedding-day came round, the Giant's daughter knew what it was that she must do.

Before the marriage took place, the King held a grand feast, to which all the people round about were invited. The old shoemaker and his wife went along with the Giant's daughter, and soon they were seated at one of the long tables in the great hall, eating and drinking and enjoying good fellowship to their hearts' content. There were many among the company who noticed the Giant's daughter, remarking on her beauty and wondering who she might be. The Prince sat with his new bride and all his kindred at the high table; and he, too, noticed the lovely maiden with the red-gold hair. A faint memory seemed to pass through his mind as he looked upon her; but if it came, then it was soon gone. Then, when the feasting and gaiety was at its height, the King called upon the company to drink to the happiness of his son, and his guests rose to their feet, wishing well to their handsome young prince.

But when the Giant's daughter raised her cup to drink to the happiness of her husband, a bright flame sprang up before it touched her lips; and everyone in that great hall fell silent, hushed into stillness by this marvellous sight. And as they watched, two pigeons rose out of the flame. The wings of the first pigeon shone with a golden light, and its breast heaved with the movement of molten gold. The other pigeon had plumage that gleamed like beaten silver; and together the birds circled through the air and alighted on the high table, directly in front of the Prince. As he watched them in amazement, they spoke to him in the human tongue.

'Oh, king's son,' said the golden one, 'do you not remember how the byre that stands in the Giant's courtyard was cleaned, and how you were delivered from your trouble?'

'Oh, king's son,' said the silver one, 'have you forgotten how that same byre was thatched with the feathers of a million birds?'

And 'Oh, king's son,' they said together, 'do you not remember how the magpies' nest in the fir-tree by the loch was harried for you? Your true love lost her little finger when you brought it down, and she wants it still.'

The Prince started to his feet, his fists clenched to his temples. He remembered the tasks the Giant had set him; he remembered how they had been accomplished; he remembered the lovely maiden he had won for his wife. Then he glanced down upon the long tables that filled the hall, and found himself looking straight into the beautiful eyes of the Giant's daughter herself. With a glad cry of joy he went to her and took her by the hand: and so the two of them were happy together at last.

The feasting and the drinking continued for days and days, and if they have not finished by now, then they are at it still.

TALES FROM THE
Episode of the Fians

The Beginning of the Fians

SCOTLAND is a country of many heroes; and the greatest remembered in the land is one of very ancient fame, whose mighty feats have been passed on by the old story-tellers for countless generations.

Fionn Mac Chumail was the leader of a band of nine thousand warriors known as the Host of the Fians, who belonged to both Eirinn and Alba, as Ireland and Scotland were called in those far-distant days; and there is scarcely an acre of land or a mountain slope in the two countries which does not hold some memory of his deeds.

The Host of the Fians was set up at a time when the Lochlannaich, or Norwegians, were harrying the coasts of Eirinn and Alba. The King of Eirinn sought counsel to discover how he should overcome his enemies; and the advice he got was to marry the hundred mightiest men and women in the land, and let their children's children form an invincible army to fight the Lochlannaich.

In this way, a generation of warriors of gigantic strength was born. The breath of their nostrils was the breath of battle; and under the leadership of Fionn they drove away the Lochlannaich and spent their time protecting the land from further attacks, and making the countryside their hunting-ground.

Fionn, although a mighty man, was not the strongest of his nine thousand warriors; but he was looked up to for his great wisdom, his generosity, his protection of the weak and defenceless, and his immaculate honour. There is a saying, ' Fionn never forsook his right-hand friend ', and all the Host of the Fians put their utmost trust in him. Fionn had a magic oracle tooth which, when he pressed it with his forefinger, gave him superhuman knowledge, and was of immeasurable use to him in his leadership of the Fians.

He had two sons: Osgar and Oisean. Osgar was called ' Chief of Men ', and performed deeds worthy of his great father. The only tears that Fionn ever shed were for the death of Osgar.

Oisean was the poet of the Fians, and, last of his race, he was left behind long after they had vanished from the earth. Old, blind, and wretched, he wandered through the land sorrowfully singing of their departed splendour.

Auburn-haired Diarmaid, ' The Expert Shield ', was another great hero of the Fians. He was the son of Fionn's twin sister, and is said to be the progenitor of the Clan Campbell: the fierce-tusked boar surmounting their crest commemorates Diarmaid's hunting in the Forest of Kintail.

Conan, Master of Fionn's hounds, was the most fiery-natured of the Fians. There was the strength of a man in him for every hair in his head; and in order to safeguard his fellow-warriors from his savage outbursts of rage, Fionn decreed that his head should be kept closely cropped.

Goll was the strongest man of the Fians: it is said of him that he could eat seven stags for his dinner.

Caolite, or 'Thinman', was the swiftest runner. When he was in full flight, he appeared as three people, so fast did he travel.

These are a few of the chief heroes of the Fians; and the following stories tell of the parts they played in some of the exploits of the legendary warrior host.

Fionn's Journey to Lochlan

ON a day soon after the Lochlannaich had been driven from the land, Fionn and his warriors were hunting deer upon the hill-side when they saw a stranger coming towards them, who saluted them in the tongue of one unfamiliar with their speech.

'Where do you come from, and what do you want of us?' Fionn asked, while his great hound Bran crouched by his side, regarding the stranger with watchful eyes—Bran, the best hunting-dog who ever lived, with his yellow paws, his two black flanks and white belly, and his two sharp, erect red ears.

'I am a lad who has come from a far distance, seeking a master,' replied the stranger.

'I am needing a lad to serve me,' said Fionn. 'What reward would you ask of me if I agreed to let you serve me for a day and a year?'

'It is not much I would ask,' replied the stranger. 'Only this: that at the end of the day and the year you will come with me to a feast and a night's entertainment at the palace of the King of Lochlan. And that you will

178

come alone, unaccompanied by either a dog, a man, a calf, a child, or any weapon.'

Fionn gave the stranger a great clap on the shoulder that sent him staggering half-way down the hill-side.

' I like your terms well,' he declared, ' for I smell adventure in them. Serve me for a day and a year, and I will go with you to Lochlan as you ask.'

For a day and a year the stranger served Fionn faithfully; and when the time of his service was over, he came to Fionn and reminded him of his promise. Then Fionn called together his nine thousand warriors under the mighty rafters of his dwelling-place and said:

' I must go now and fulfil my bond to this lad. I do not know when I shall return; but if I am not back within a year and a day, then you will know that I have been murdered by the Lochlannaich; and if this should come to pass, let the man of you who will not be whetting his sword be bending his bow for the purpose of holding one great day on the strand of Lochlan, avenging my death.'

As he passed through the door-posts of his dwelling, his Fool cried out to him and said:

' Oh, Fionn, leader of men, take heed of my advice, for the wisdom of a King has often been lodged in the head of a Fool.'

' What is your advice ? ' asked Fionn.

' It is this. Take with you on your journey Bran's chain of gold. It is neither a dog, a man, a calf, a child, nor a weapon, and yet it may be of great use to you.'

' I will do this,' said Fionn; and putting Bran's chain in his pocket, he departed from his people, following in the steps of the lad who had been his servant.

Though Fionn was swift and speedy, he found that the lad was faster yet, and he had a great trouble to keep him in sight as they travelled through the countryside, over

bracken slopes and bogs, across rivers and lochs.   When
the lad would be going out of sight at one mountain gap,
Fionn would be just coming round the one before it,
and they kept up this pace until they reached the end of
their journey: the palace of the King of Lochlan.

Black and grim, it stood overlooking the sea strand
where foaming breakers snarled round the cliffs.   Wearied
with his journey, and eager for the feast that had been
promised him, Fionn went into the palace and sat down in
a chair to rest himself.   But there was to be no feast for
Fionn Mac Chumail that day.   Instead, he found the
King of Lochlan and all his black-browed chiefs and
nobles putting their heads together to see what dis-
graceful death they could bring upon him.   Once inside
the palace he became their prisoner, and he knew that
they would show no mercy towards him.

' Let us hang him ! ' urged one counsellor.

' He shall burn ! ' cried another.

' Drown him in the deepest loch of all ! ' declared a
third.

And then a man of even fiercer visage than his fellows
stood up and said :

' There is one death that will bring far greater shame
upon Fionn Mac Chumail than any of these things.   Let
us send him to the Great Glen, where lives the dreaded
Grey Dog, who will tear him mercilessly limb from limb.
There could not be another death in the world more dis-
graceful in the minds of the Fians than that their leader
should fall by a cur of a dog.'

At these words, a great cheering and clapping arose
from the assembly, for no one there could think of a
worse or more terrifying death than to perish in the cruel
jaws of the monstrous Grey Dog, who had roamed the
Great Glen for many years, claiming as his victims all
who wandered in his way.

Without delay they rose up and went from the palace to the Glen, and here, amid a misty wilderness of black thorn trees and craggy rocks, with the baying of the sharp-fanged Dog sounding in the distance, they left Fionn alone.

Now staying where he was and running away were all one to Fionn; for if he ran back the way he had come he would be put to death by his enemies, and if he stayed where he was he would be killed by the Dog. And as it seemed to him to be a better thing to fall by the Dog than by the hand of the treacherous Lochlannaich, he remained still as he heard the howling of the beast sounding ever louder, prepared to face death in the manner of a hero.

Suddenly through the mist he saw the Grey Dog there before him; and in spite of all, his knees trembled and he shook with fear. The Dog was as huge as Bran himself, and the hackles along his back stood up like spearheads. His mouth was open, and his red tongue hung over two rows of pointed fangs. Each snort from his nostrils scorched all that lay within a distance of three miles before him and around him, and Fionn felt his skin shrivel in the dreadful heat.

At that moment he remembered that Bran's gold chain lay in his pocket, where he had placed it on the advice of his Fool. A last hope came to him, and he took out the chain and held it before him, shaking it up and down. Instantly, just as though some enchantment had fallen on him, the Grey Dog stood still, stopped his howling, and began to wag his tail. Then he approached Fionn and licked him all over from the top of his head to the sole of his foot, until he had healed with his tongue all the sore places that were burnt with his scorching breath. At last Fionn clapped Bran's chain about the Grey Dog's neck, and then went on through the Glen, with the beast meekly walking by his side.

At the lower end of the Glen there was a cottage where an Old Woman lived with her husband; and she happened to be standing by the door when Fionn came by with the Grey Dog. At such a strange sight she sprang inside the cottage, wailing and beating her hands.

'What is it? What have you seen?' asked her husband.

'The tallest and most splendid man in the world is coming through the Glen with the terrible Grey Dog himself held in a leash of gold,' she told him.

'There is only one in all the world who could do such a thing,' replied the Old Man. 'And that is Fionn Mac Chumail. And the leash you speak of is Bran's chain of gold.'

Then he rose and went outside the cottage to greet Fionn, who told him what had passed in the Great Glen. The kind couple made him welcome in their home, and the Old Man said:

'The reason why the Grey Hound lost his savagery at the sight of Bran's chain of gold is that he was born a brother to Bran, and was reared with him in one litter. And even as Bran will follow you faithfully to the end of his days, so this Grey Hound acknowledges you as his master.'

Fionn marvelled at this stroke of fortune which had preserved his life, and praised the Old Man for his great knowledge. The Old Man and his wife for their part rejoiced in Fionn's company, and bade him remain in their house for as long as he pleased.

Fionn found that life went by very pleasantly in the cottage by the Great Glen, and gladly availed himself of their hospitality. So pleasantly did life go by that it seemed but a little moment before a year and a day had passed: a year and a day since Fionn left the Host of the Fians for Lochlan.

At the end of this time, the Old Woman was standing on a knoll near by the cottage when she beheld an amazing sight on the strand below. She ran quickly into the cottage, her eyes wide with amazement.

' There is a countless host of gigantic warriors gathered together on the strand ! ' she cried. ' And at their head there is a red-haired man whose match in combat cannot be beneath the stars.'

At her words, Fionn leapt to his feet with joy.

' They are the companies of my love ! ' he cried, ' and the warrior whom you describe is my son Osgar. I must go forth to meet them ! '

And straightway he went down to the strand, and the Grey Dog sprang up from the chimney corner to accompany him. When the Host of the Fians saw him coming before them, alive and hale, they raised a great shout of rejoicing that was heard in the four corners of Lochlan. And if the welcome between Fionn and his followers was joyful, no less joyful was the greeting between Bran and his brother the Grey Dog.

' We had come with whetted swords and bent bows to avenge your death, father,' said Osgar. ' For it is a year and a day since you left us, and we thought that surely you had been killed.'

' No, my son, I am alive,' replied Fionn. ' But it is not the fault of the Lochlannaich that I am not dead.'

And he told his men of the treacherous plot that had been carried out against him by the King of Lochlan and his followers.

Then Fionn and all the Host of the Fians drew their swords and put arrows to their bows, and took a terrible vengeance upon the men of Lochlan, so that the strand grew red with blood, and a dreadful sound of lamentation overcame the thunder of the surf upon the shore. And when it was over, they returned to their own country and held a great feast of triumph.

And from that day the Grey Dog joined the hounds of the Fians.

The Death of Diarmaid

THERE came a time when Fionn desired to take a wife; and although there were many lovely women who would gladly have consented to marry him, he decided that she whom he chose must be as wise and quick-witted as she was beautiful. To measure wit and wisdom, Fionn devised six questions which he put to every woman he visited; and he declared that she who could answer his questions should be his wife.

Now the Earl of Ullin had a daughter called Grainne, whose beauty was famed throughout the countryside; and it was Grainne of the dark hair and lovely eyes who gave Fionn the answers to his six questions, when he came visiting her father's house.

'What is more plenteous than the grass?' Fionn asked her.

'The dew-drops,' Grainne replied; 'for there will be many drops of dew upon one grass blade.'

'What is whiter than the snow?' asked Fionn.

'There is truth,' Grainne replied.

'What is blacker than the raven?' he asked.

' There is death,' she replied.

' What is redder than blood ? '

' The face of a worthy man when strangers chance to enter his house, and he has no meat to offer them.'

' What is sharper than the sword ? '

' The reproach of an enemy.'

' And what is swifter than the wind ? '

' A woman's thought between two men,' Grainne answered; and each of her replies were made without a moment's hesitation.

Then Fionn took both her hands in his.

' Truly, Grainne,' he said, ' of all women your beauty shines brightest, and your wit is quickest. Will you be my wife ? '

' To be the wife of Fionn Mac Chumail is the best honour that could befall me,' she answered.

So a splendid wedding-feast was prepared in the great hall of the Earl of Ullin's house; and all the nine thousand warrior heroes in the Host of the Fians came to rejoice at the marriage of their great leader. The rafters of the roof trembled at the thunder of their laughter; and the walls shook with the clash of their drinking-cups; and the feasting and merry-making continued for seven days.

Among the nine thousand heroes assembled there was Diarmaid, Fionn's nephew, and after Fionn and Osgar the third best hero in the Fians. Now Diarmaid of the auburn hair was the most handsome man of all his fellows; and high up on his left cheekbone he had a love spot which he kept always covered; for if any woman should catch a glimpse of it, so powerful was its charm that she would instantly fall in love with him. When the feasting was at its height, Grainne's two white hounds, who crouched by her chair, fell to fighting over a bone that had been tossed to the ground; and immediately

Diarmaid leapt up to separate them. And this little action spelt the beginning of all the sorrow that fell upon him from that day. For as he knelt to force the hounds apart, the covering fell from his cheekbone, and Grainne saw the love spot there, and instantly fell in love with him.

'Fionn is a wise and mighty leader,' she thought, 'and he has greatly honoured me. But Diarmaid is most handsome of all men, and there is the light of youth in his eyes. It is Diarmaid I love.'

And later, when Fionn was heavy with wine and half-asleep in his chair, with his head bowed to his heart, Grainne leant across and told Diarmaid of her love.

'Let us flee from this place together!' she implored him. 'Take me with you tonight, and we will go where Fionn will never find us.'

Now Grainne's great beauty had put upon Diarmaid a charm equal in power to that of his own love spot; but although her words sorely tempted him, he swore that he could never betray Fionn and steal away his bride.

'Would you have me most dishonoured of all the Fians?' he asked her.

'I am putting *geasan* on thee to go with me,' she answered.

When she said this, Diarmaid sighed a great sigh, for in those far-off days it was ordained that if a woman put *geasan* upon a man, he was bound to do whatever she asked him. Yet still seeking a means whereby he need not denounce his loyalty to Fionn, Diarmaid said:

'O Grainne, heavy is the fate you would place upon me. I will take you away from here as you command me, but this shall be the only manner of our going:

'I will not take thee within doors, and I will not take thee without. I will not take thee on horseback, neither will I take thee on foot. And unless thou canst show me how this shall be accomplished, we will not go at all.'

And forthwith he rose from the table and went into a nearby house.

In the morning, Grainne came to this house with her two white hounds following behind her, and called:

'Diarmaid, come forth. For you may see how I have fulfilled the conditions of our going.'

And when Diarmaid arose, he saw that she had indeed fulfilled all his conditions. For she was neither on horseback nor on foot, but was mounted on a buck-goat; and she was neither within doors nor without, but stayed between the doorposts of the house.

'Truly, Fionn knew well that you are the most quick-witted as well as the loveliest of all women,' said Diarmaid; 'and it is time for our departure. Yet I fear that wherever we shall flee, there is no place where we may go that Fionn will not discover us. For he has only to put his forefinger to his tooth of knowledge, and our hiding-place will be made known to him. His anger will be terrible, and he will not rest until he has brought down vengeance upon my head.'

Then Grainne dismounted from the goat, and accompanied by the two white hounds, they set off with great speed across the land, never resting the soles of their feet until there was a distance of many green hills and valleys between them and the house of the Earl of Ullin, and they reached the pleasant countryside of Kintyre. But fast as was their flight, faster yet was Fionn's pursuit; for as soon as he found out that Diarmaid had departed with his bride, he pressed his magic tooth with his forefinger, and immediately the knowledge that the two fugitives had reached Kintail leapt into his mind. Then he and all the Host of the Fians made ready, and went from Ullin to Kintyre; and their pace was the pace of Fionn's furious anger.

'Never would I have thought that Diarmaid, who held a chief place in my heart, would have betrayed me thus,' said Fionn; and the knotty veins in his neck bulged with fury. At length they reached a high hill-top overlooking the great forest of Kintail, where Fionn unslung his hunting-horn and blew a great blast upon it that sounded throughout the length and breadth of the land.

Now each warrior of the Fians was sworn to answer Fionn's *foghaid*, or hunting-cry; and when Diarmaid heard the sound of the horn, he knew that he must obey its call.

'There is no help for it, beloved,' he told Grainne. 'I am under bonds to answer the call of the *foghaid*, and I must go before Fionn.'

And when she saw that he was determined to go, Grainne said:

'I will come with you, beloved. And if there is death in Fionn's heart for you, there may my death lie also.'

Then they rose up and met Fionn upon the high hill-top, where he stood with Osgar and Oisean and the chief heroes of his band, while Bran the faithful crouched by his side. When Fionn saw Diarmaid and Grainne approaching him, hand in hand, the anger in his heart died away a little.

'Diarmaid is very young for death,' he thought. Then the thought of his nephew's treachery returned in full force. 'But die he must,' he decided; and because he shrank from the thought of cutting down Diarmaid with his own sword, he devised another plan whereby he could accomplish his revenge.

In Kintail forest there lived an old woman called Mala Llee, or Grey Eyebrow, who kept a herd of swine guarded by a venomous boar. Many heroes had gone forth to hunt this boar, but none had returned, so savage was its attack. The plan that now entered Fionn's head was to send Diarmaid to hunt the boar; thus would he accomplish his nephew's death and satisfy his own desire for revenge.

He saluted Diarmaid and told him what he must do; and, knowing that he was surely going to his death, Diarmaid bade farewell to Osgar and Oisean, his cousins and the friends of his youth; he took a grave leave of Fionn; and last of all he said good-bye to Grainne the beautiful. Then he picked up his spear and went down the hill into the forest, vanishing through the leafy foliage.

Soon those waiting on the hill-top knew that Diarmaid had found his quarry, for to their ears there came the distant sound of his struggle with the boar; they heard a crashing and charging amid the undergrowth, and the beast's furious snorts of rage. Then suddenly there was silence; and then, borne clearly to their ears, there came a shout of human triumph. Diarmaid had killed the boar.

Straightway Fionn and his sons rushed into the forest; and there they found Diarmaid unharmed, resting by the side of the boar, which lay lifeless on the ground, its black blood gushing from a hundred thrusts of the hunter's spear.

'Not for nothing do men call you Diarmaid the Expert Shield,' Fionn told his nephew; but behind his words of praise he felt great anger that his plan had not succeeded.

Now Fionn knew that a number of poisonous bristles grew along the boar's back, one prick of which would kill a man; and so he called to Diarmaid and said:

'Measure your prize, my nephew; walk along its back and tell me how many feet there are from snout to tail.'

Diarmaid, suspecting nothing, stood up and measured the boar bare-footed, as Fionn bade him; and by good fortune he did not tread on any of the poisonous spikes.

'Sixteen feet of measure true,' he called when he had finished.

'Measure it again lest you are mistaken,' Fionn commanded him; and so Diarmaid re-paced the beast's

broad back. But half-way along one of the fatal bristles pierced a mole on his right heel, and straightway the deadly poison entered his body and he fell dying to the ground.

Then Fionn was smitten with remorse and cried out:

'Diarmaid! What will make you well again?'

And Diarmaid answered feebly: 'A draught of water from the palms of Fionn.'

Immediately Fionn went to a stream that splashed among the trees, and scooped some water into his hands. But as he did so, the memory of his great anger when he first discovered that Diarmaid had fled with Grainne came back to him, and he let the water trickle out through his fingers. Yet again he filled his cupped palms to overflowing; but, torn between his old love for Diarmaid and furious anger at his betrayal, once more the precious water trickled away; and by the time that he finally returned to his nephew's side, Diarmaid was dead.

' I have killed my sister's only son for the sake of a woman who no longer loves me,' mourned Fionn. ' He who was the third best hero of the Fians has fallen by my hand.'

Then Osgar and Oisean, Goll the Strong, Conan of the Hounds—all who had grown up with Diarmaid and shared their youth with him—mourned him bitterly. But when Grainne knew that Diarmaid was dead, her spirit failed within her, and she, too, died for grief of being alone.

And by Loch Duich, beside the grey, still waters, they buried Diarmaid and Grainne together, with all honour. They laid their bodies in Diarmaid's long galley, and about them they placed his spear, his sharp-edged sword, his famous shield, and all his personal possessions. And at Grainne's feet they placed her two white hounds, who also died of loneliness. Then they built a great mound to mark their grave, which is to this day known as the Dirman Diarmaid.

How Fionn found his Sword

AFTER the death of Diarmaid, the Fians crossed over from Kintyre and went hunting on Islay. And as Fionn bestrode the hill-side brandishing his long-hafted spear, a broad-shouldered, swarthy stranger who had but one eye in the middle of his forehead came leaping over the turf towards him.

' Fionn Mac Chumail, leader of men, will you not follow me to the door of my smithy ? ' he asked in a ringing voice.

' Surely you are no mortal smith,' Fionn answered him. ' Yet I will follow if you will lead the way.'

Then the faery smith gave a wild laugh that echoed across the hills.

' Follow if you can, Fionn Mac Chumail ! ' he cried; and at once he set off with the terrible speed of the storm-wind, while Fionn followed at his heels.

They crossed that hill-side and the next; they took one mighty stride over each desert glen; they stayed but a step in every valley; and the mountain grass shook with the speed of their passing. And never once did Fionn fall behind, or slacken his furious pace.

At last they reached a stone cabin that stood at the

head of a stony pass; and here the faery smith turned and shook Fionn by the hand.

'We are well matched in speed,' he said. 'This is my smithy, and we will now go in together and forge a sword worthy of your wielding.'

They entered the cabin, where the smith's daughter gave them a glad welcome; and while Fionn blew up the fire, the smith took a great bar of iron and forged from it a hero's sword.

When it was almost finished, and the two-handled hilt had been fitted to the blade, the smith's daughter came to Fionn and whispered to him as he plied the bellows, the sweat pouring down his brow in the tremendous heat of the fire.

'Thy sword is almost finished, Fionn,' she told him. 'Soon my father will turn to you and say: "What else is there left to do?" Then you must answer him: "The sword is wanting but one little thing yet"—and, seizing it in your hand, thrust it through his body. And because it is tempered in his blood, this sword will be the mightiest ever made.'

Fionn listened to her counsel; and sure enough, in a little while the faery smith turned to him and said:

'Now, Fionn, the sword is almost finished. What else is there left to do?'

Whereupon Fionn leapt to his feet, grasped the hilt in both hands, and drove the sharp blade through rib and backbone. Then he put one foot upon the body of the smith, withdrew the blade, and went from the house to rejoin his men.

Thus tempered in the blood of the faery smith, the great two-handled sword was indeed the mightiest ever made, for wherever it struck it found its mark, and left not a shred behind. The name of the sword was Mac an Luinne, and from that day it never left Fionn's side.

Conan's Punishment

IT happened one year that a time of scarce hunting
came to the Fians. The flesh fell away from their
ribs, and the cheekbones protruded from their faces;
and at last, despairing of their luck in Islay, they returned
to Ardnamurchan, where they had left their wives, in-
tending to pursue the chase there instead.

What was the astonishment of the nine thousand
heroes to find their wives plump and well nourished in
this lean time; they were twice as comely as before, and
never complained of hunger.

The men of the Fians discussed this wonder among
themselves; and at last Fionn said:

'It is shame upon us, providers of the chase, that our
womenfolk are able to find food when we cannot. Let
us not humble ourselves to beg their secret from them,
but let one of us stay behind to find it out without their
knowledge, while his fellows hunt in Skye tomorrow.'

Then he turned to Conan, Master of his Hounds, and
said:

'You shall discover the mystery of this matter for us,
Conan, and reveal it to us on our return.'

Conan agreed to this willingly; and when his companions set off for Skye in the mouth of the next day's morning, he stayed behind and concealed himself in the branches of a tree to watch the women.

By and by they came out to prepare their first meal; and Conan saw them scatter to the hill-side to collect heather roots, fern plants, and sweet hazel tops. These they flung into their great cooking-pot, and lit a fire beneath it; and before long a succulent smell arose from the simmering broth, that wafted its way through the air and tickled Conan's nostrils, so that he sneezed a mighty sneeze, which dislodged him from his tree-branch. Down he fell with a tremendous thump into the midst of the women.

When they realized how he had concealed himself to spy upon them, the women were filled with anger against him.

' Had our menfolk forgotten their stiff pride and asked us our secret, we would gladly have told it to them,' they said. ' But instead, you must steal it from us like thieves.'

Yet because they feared Conan's fiery outbursts of rage, especially since his head, which, you will remember, held the strength of a man in every hair, had not been cropped since the famine began, they said no more, but gave him some of the broth to drink.

But when Conan lay down to rest himself after he had eaten, with his hunger satisfied as it had not been for many days, they whispered among themselves and decided upon a plan to punish him for his curiosity.

They drove two stakes of wood into the earth on either side of his head where he lay, and about the stakes they twisted his long hair. Then they went away a little distance, and made a great noise of shouting and wailing. Their clamour woke Conan with a start; and thinking that an enemy was at hand, or that some other calamity had fallen on the women, he leapt to his feet on the instant that he opened his eyes.

Immediately he let forth an agonized scream, for his hair was so tightly bound to the stakes that the skin of his head was torn away, and blood streamed over his shoulders. Maddened with pain, a black fit of rage came over him and, falling upon the women, he herded them all into one little cabin. Then he set a huge pile of brushwood and faggots before the doorway and set fire to it, so that his tormentors would be suffocated with the smoke.

But scarcely had the flames licked the underlying brushwood when one of the Fians paused in his hill-side hunting on Skye and looked across the intervening strip of water to Ardnamurchan shore.

'What is that rising column of smoke I see?' he asked. 'Surely danger threatens our womenfolk.'

Filled with fear, all the Fians immediately abandoned the hunt and set off to succour their wives. One bound they gave from the hill-side to the shore; and then they put their long-hafted spears before them and, balanced on their points, leapt over the width of water that separated them from the mainland. One hero fell by the way; he tumbled from his spear in mid-air, and the waters closed over his head for ever. His name was Mac An Reaidhinn, and ever since, the strait between Skye and that part of the mainland has been called Caol Reaidhinn, or Kyle Ray.

But his fellow warriors, with Fionn himself at their head, reached the other side in safety; and as soon as they reached the cabin where Conan had trapped their wives, they destroyed the fire he had built, trampling the smouldering brushwood underfoot and pulling away the flaming faggots with their bare hands.

Their wives rushed out from the cabin with tears of joy streaming down their cheeks; and when Fionn heard their story, he turned to Conan and decreed the punishment he must pay.

'There is death for thee, hot-tempered Conan,' he declared. 'That is the penalty which justice demands.'

Then Conan fell to his knees before Fionn, while his fellow warriors stood round about in silence.

'Since death is my due, mighty Fionn,' he cried, 'grant me but this: that my beheading may be accomplished with the sharp edge of Mac an Luinne, which never leaves a shred behind. And let my death stroke be given by my own son, Garbh, as my head lies on Fionn's thigh.'

This request Fionn granted Conan; and though he felt a great horror rise up in him, young Garbh prepared to obey his father's wish. Then Fionn took seven thick hides, and seven faggots of firewood, and seven strips of grey tree bark, and bound them about his thigh, to protect himself from the sharp edge of Mac an Luinne. And when this was done, Conan came and laid his head on Fionn's thigh, and Garbh took up the great two-handled sword. With a gleam of steel and a rush of air it came down and severed Conan's head from his body in one clean cut; and in spite of the seven-fold protection wrapped about Fionn's thigh, blood spurted from his arteries and ran on to the heather.

Then Garbh screamed to see his father's head struck off, and he went mad.

'Where are the Fians? Where are my comrades?' he cried, not recognizing those about him. 'Surely they will avenge Conan's death.'

When they beheld the madness that had fallen upon Garbh, his companions told him that the Host of the Fians had descended to the bottom of the sea; and wildly crying upon the name of Fionn, he ran down to the shore and was drowned.

.   .   .   .   .

Soon after these happenings, the Fians' arrows found the deer again, and their hunting-spears pierced the wild boars' flesh once more, and so the great famine was over.

The Green Isle

WHAT became of the Fians when the whole tale of their mighty deeds was told, and they departed from the earth? Some say that Fionn and all his warrior host fell in a great battle, and died as mortal men must die. They point to a hill in Perthshire which is known as Cill Fhinn, or Fionn's Tomb, and to a boat-shaped mound called Tom-na-h-iuchraich at Glenurchy, in Inverness, where his heroes are said to lie buried.

There are others who say that Fionn did not die, but that he lives still on a green island at the extremity of the Uttermost World. The name of this far-western isle is *Eilean na h-oige*, the Island of Youth; here grow the magic Avlan apples, and here is found the health-restoring water from the springs of life. Blessed are they who reach this Celtic paradise, the Land of Light and Heart's Desire; for if the sole of their foot once touches the shore, they become as they were at twenty years old: their bent limbs straighten, their grey hairs vanish, and their wrinkles pass away.

This is a story about a man who did set foot upon this

isle. He lived in Jura, in the Inner Hebrides, and his name was Angus MacGregor. He owned a small sailing-vessel, and carried cargoes between the islands and the mainland. One day he was standing upon Greenock Pier when he saw coming towards him the biggest man he had ever set eyes on. He was three heads and shoulders above all the other people there, and he had a flaming red beard that blazed down to his chest. He gave Angus a great clap on the shoulder and said:

' They tell me you have a vessel that will carry cargo between the islands and the mainland. I have a cargo of meat to take to an island west of Islay; will you carry me over with it? '

Then they agreed to terms, and the big man brought his cargo to Angus' vessel. Great was Angus' astonishment when he saw the enormous carcasses of beef and mutton that went aboard his boat.

' Surely there is enough meat to provision an army of Highlanders,' he thought.

When all was ready, Angus hoisted his sails and they began their journey according to the big man's direction. Away they went up the Firth of Clyde, past Arran, round the Mull of Kintyre, and through the Sound of Islay. Then a thick fog came down upon the waters, and steering blindly, Angus did as the big man bade him, and bore farther westward yet. For two days they saw not a blink of land or sky; and Angus, wondering where they were, thought to himself:

' It must be that we have passed the uttermost bounds of the Outer Hebrides.'

On the third day the fog lifted, and Angus saw that they were nearing the shore of an island he had never seen before. Surrounded by the grey, still sea, it appeared to him as a green haven promising rest and peacefulness.

' That is the end of our journey,' said the big man.

Angus saw that it would be some time yet before they reached the shore; and so he went below to take a short sleep. It was the gentle bumping of the boat against the shore-side that awoke him; and he arose to discover that he was riding high out of the water, for the cargo of meat had been unloaded, and of the big man there was no trace.

Now it had been agreed that Angus should be paid for the journey when they reached their destination; and when he found that he had been cheated of his money, he was determined to find out where the big man had gone.

So he stepped off his boat and waded through the shallows to the grassy shore. And as soon as he stood on the island, it was as though a weight was lifted from his shoulders; all the signs of his age tumbled from him, and he became as he was at twenty years old.

He marvelled at the lightness in his step, and felt his smooth forehead in wonder.

' It is *Eilean na h-oige*,' he breathed, ' the Island of Everlasting Youth.'

Then he realized that the big man he had carried in his ship must be one of the Fians themselves.

' For men of his mightiness do not walk the earth today,' he said. ' And so it is also *Flath-innis-ean*, the Heroes' Isle.'

But even so, he was still determined to get the wages for his journey from Greenock; and he went on his way inland. Before long he reached a great house built of enormous stones. The doorway was twenty feet high, and the lintel twenty feet broad, and he stepped inside to find himself in a vast hall where a huge, big-boned old man whose beard reached to his knees sat alone in a massive chair.

His countenance bore the grim stamp of a thousand battles, and in his eyes there was everlasting sorrow for those brave heroes who had fallen as they fought by his side. It was Fionn Mac Chumail. Presently he turned and saw Angus.

' What is thy business here ? ' he asked him.

Then he raised his great hand.

' First you must drink, and then tell me your story,' he said; and he held out to Angus a huge drinking-vessel filled with golden mead.

It was so heavy that Angus used all his strength to raise it with both hands to his lips; and when he had finished drinking, he set it down and told Fionn his story.

Then Fionn said: ' Tell me, thou man of Jura, would you be able to recognize this big man who left you without paying you your due, if he came before you now ? '

' I would,' Angus replied.

So Fion called out in a mighty voice, and at once the hall began to fill with heroes whose limbs were as tree-trunks, and whose tread shook the floor beneath their feet. And among them, Angus saw the big man whom he had brought over the water from Greenock. It was an easy enough matter to recognize him, for who could mistake that great flaming beard ?

' That is the man,' he told Fionn.

Then Fionn ordered the big man to pay what was due to Angus, which he did with a bad grace. And when he had handed over the money, and after Fionn had bade his visitor farewell, he met Angus as he came through the doorway of the hall, and, seizing him by the shoulder, put out his right eye with his finger.

' If I had done that to thee before, thou wouldst not have known me,' he said.

In great pain, and with blood streaming from his eye-socket, Angus stumbled down to the shore, accompanied on his way by the big man. When they reached the place where the boat lay anchored, the big man turned to Angus and bade him shake every particle of the dust of the island from his feet.

Then Angus went aboard his boat once more, and set sail for home. As he went away, it seemed that the green island disappeared in a mist that rose up from the waters; and when it had utterly passed from view, the weight of all his years descended on him once more.

And all he ever had to show for his journey to *Eilean na h-oige* was the loss of his right eye.

The Fians Asleep in the Great Rock

THERE is yet another tradition concerning Fionn Mac Chumail, which says that he sleeps with his companions of the battle and the chase in a great rock that stands in Skye. And those who believe this legend say that the mighty hero and his warriors will rise again in all their ancient strength if either of two things come to pass.

If anyone should enter the great rock and blow three blasts upon the Wooden-Crier that lies by Fionn's side, or if twenty-four hours should go by and the tale of the Fians' fame remains unspoken of, then they will wake again. (Yet some who once fought and hunted by Fionn's side will not arise; for Osgar perished in the heat of battle, and Oisean, spirited away from his companions in the days of his youth, returned long after they were gone, and lived out his life alone, as a blind old man. Nor will Diarmaid of the auburn hair awake; or Conan, whose fiery nature brought about his downfall.)

Now the name of this great rock is the Smith's Rock, and the reason is this.

There was once a Smith of Skye who, having learnt

the legend of the rock, resolved that he would attempt to enter it and wake the Fians. One day he rose up and made his way over the hill-side until he reached the rock; and here he discovered a passage that led far back into its very centre, where it widened into a massive chamber whose roof and walls were lost in shadows.

And in the strange half-light the Smith could see a company of gigantic men stretched out upon the ground. Here were the Fians, with the sleep of a thousand years upon their eyelids. Their limbs were as huge as tree-trunks, and their features were set in stern, grim lines. About them lay their helmets and weapons; shields of giant size, spears as tall as pine-saplings, and swords whose brightness was undimmed.

The mightiest one of all lay in the centre of his comrades; and by his outstretched fingers lay a huge, hollow wooden baton. As soon as he set eyes on him, the Smith knew that this was Fionn Mac Chumail himself, with his Wooden-Crier close to his grasp. For a long time he stood still, daunted by the presence of the mighty heroes all about him; heroes whose great deeds had been recounted to him by the old story-tellers since he was a little child, and whose names were as familiar to his tongue as those of his own people. At last he told himself that, having come so far, he must attempt that which he had set out to do; and with a sudden vision of the great ones returned in glory to the land, he bent to raise the Wooden-Crier to his mouth.

Now the Smith was accounted among his neighbours as a man of great strength; yet it was all he could do to lift one end of that Wooden-Crier which Fionn had so often held to his lips between two fingers—that Wooden-Crier which he blew if he was ever in a death-strait. Its sound would pass through the seven borders of the earth, and to the extremity of the Uttermost World. Then the

Smith summoned all his strength and blew a blast upon it; and so loud was the sound it produced that the walls of the rock seemed to shiver, and the ground to shake beneath his feet.

The huge heroes quivered in their sleep from the tops of their heads to the soles of their feet; and perhaps some dim memory of that sonorous call as they had heard it of old stirred their blood anew.

Again the Smith gathered his breath and blew upon the Crier a second time; and with one movement the Fians turned on their sides, and raised themselves on their elbows. And with terror, the Smith saw that their eyes had opened.

' Alas ! What have I done ! ' he cried; and such a wild panic came upon him that he threw away the Wooden-Crier and fled back to the passage that led to the daylight. Then a sound of many voices pursued him; and they were crying with terrible sorrow:

' Worse have you left us than you found us, worse have you left us than you found us . . .'

But the Smith did not once look back; and reaching the open hill-side, he never stopped running until he was safely inside his own house, where he bolted fast the door and vowed that never again would he form such a foolhardy resolution as that which had led him to the great rock.